Prayers That Avail Much for Women

Special Gift Edition

James 5:16

Prayers That Avail Much for Women

Special Gift Edition

James 5:16

And this is the confidence that we have in him, that, if we ask any thing according to his will, he heareth us: and if we know that he hear us, whatsoever we ask, we know that we have the petitions that we desired of him.

1 John 5:14,15

Harrison House
Tulsa, Oklahoma

Calligraphy by Victoria Lane

Prayers That Avail Much for Women, Special Gift Edition
ISBN 1-57794-127-6

Copyright © 1997 by Word Ministries, Inc.
38 Sloan Street
Roswell, Georgia 30075

2nd Printing

Published by Harrison House, Inc.
P. O. Box 35035
Tulsa, Oklahoma 74153

Presented to

Candy

By

Mom

Date

5/9/99

Occasion

1ˢᵗ Mother's Day

Contents

7

Part II: Prayers for Relationships

10

A Word to Women

Dear Friend,

Welcome to the *Prayers That Avail Much Family Series.* There are many issues facing today's woman, and demands for your time may seem overwhelming. *Prayers That Avail Much for Women* is a compilation of prayers from our existing books that we believe will be helpful in scheduling and keeping your prayer appointments with God. These prayers will inspire and motivate you to achieve spiritual growth and emotional wholeness.

Developing an effectual prayer life and consistently reading the Bible enables you to become more intimately acquainted with God. You learn to recognize and understand His nature, and appreciate the value He has placed on you. The God Who created woman is the Lord Who gives the word [of power]. He calls women to bear and publish the good news, and we are a great host. (Psalm 68:11 AMP)

In the beginning when God created all things He said, "Now we will make humans, and they will be like us. We will let them rule the fish, the birds, and all other living creatures." So God created humans to be like himself; he made men and women. (Genesis 1:26-27 CEV)

What were God's intentions when He designed woman? Did God give equal power and ability to both the woman and man? Does God allow women to minister in the church? What do you believe about the woman in Proverbs 31? After attempting to be this woman, I concluded that she is a composite of God's woman describing various gifts and talents deposited within the makeup of individuals. God created you a distinctive person, and I want to encourage you to find the answers to these questions. The Holy Spirit is the One Who will guide you into all Truth — the Reality of who you are.

It takes valuable time to answer these questions. The church and society at one time were very specific in defining "WOMAN" according to her roles. In the environment where I grew up it was understood that the woman would stay in her place at home and in the church. Was this "place" God's place for her? Who decided that she was too emotional to make decisions, and that her ideas and opinions were invalid? God declares that you are a capable, intelligent, and virtuous woman more precious than jewels, and your value is far above rubies or pearls. (Proverbs 31:10) Our Lord Jesus honored women, defended women, and valued women. Jesus brought redemption to everyone — both men and women. He delivered those in bondage to sin, forgave them and restored them to wholeness.

After many years of fighting to break out of the mold designed for me by others, I came to know the

Creator as my Heavenly Father. It would require much studying, praying, and emotional healing before I quit fighting to be the "me" God created. I could not make this happen — I was not able to change me — there seemed to be no escape from my prisons of guilt, shame, fear and intimidation. God provided a way of escape where there seemed to be *no* way. My escape was in the Person of Jesus Christ. He is the Way, the Truth and the Life. In the presence of God I learned that I am free to make choices. My "today" is a result of choices I made yesterday. Spiritual growth and emotional wholeness allowed me to assume responsibility for my choices.

In *Prayers That Avail Much For Women* we have provided you a starting place. Find a quiet, peaceful space, and set aside time, preferably, at the beginning of your day to commune with God. Begin by addressing Him as "Our Father." Acknowledge His Sovereignty asking Him to hallow His Name in your personality, and in all your roles and activities. Ask for His will to be done, for His Kingdom to come in all your decisions and encounters. Make your petitions known to Him forgiving others as freely as He has forgiven you. Affirm the Lordship of Jesus and submit to the constant ministry of transformation by the Holy Spirit.

Part 1 includes prayers for personal needs. It is God's desire that you know His will for your life. In

13

God's divine providence there is healing for crippled and damaged emotions. He delivered you out of the authority of darkness and translated you into the kingdom of His dear Son. Old thought patterns are replaced with new and the metamorphosis from "victim" to "victor" becomes a reality. You are more than a conqueror through Him that loves you. Learning to live victoriously is a process that takes time. We have to train our senses to know right from wrong. You will overcome personal fears — fear of failure, of being alone, or of having to prove yourself to others. You can look in the mirror and approve of the "you" God created. He gives you the grace to come out of the snare of the enemy. You will no longer fear the opinions of man.

You were born for such a time as this. Do you know who you are? Do you know why you were born? What is your mission in life? Do you know your strengths? It seems that most of us know our weaknesses. Are you able to glory in your weaknesses allowing the power of God to prevail? Knowing the answers to these questions will give you direction and empower you to make wise decisions. As you assume responsibility for your decisions, you will reap the rewards.

Relationships are important to us, and we have a special section of prayers that will prepare you for developing healthy relationships with God, with family and with others. I meet many single women who are looking for a man to complete themselves. Concentrate on becoming the woman that God created you to be, and you will not have to expose yourself to ungodly, unholy alliances that result in guilt and condemnation.

The battered woman feels trapped, and wonders if she will ever find a way out. Some continue living with abusive men thinking that things will change — they will get better. Others have given up hope of the situation ever changing, and go from one storm to another, grateful for the lulls. The addictions and behaviors of the significant other controls their thoughts and behavior. Prayer prepares you to practice tough love, make godly decisions and necessary changes.

Often, women are angry with God for His failure to intervene in situations that they actualized by their unwise choices. They seem eager to hold onto unhealthy relationships believing that they can change the other person, willing to stay no matter how great the emotional cost to them and their children. What kind of values and standards are we teaching our children?

Women living in abusive relationships, often believe they are "right" and want God to correct the husband or significant other. On occasion a caller to our ministry becomes angry when we dare minister that God called her to peace, not to accept her husband's infidelities and endure abuses. There are several things we share with them.

- God does not require you to live with abuse. Once when the crowd wanted to throw Jesus off a cliff, He turned and walked away. Change begins with you, and change brings change. God has instructed us to put on the new nature created in Christ Jesus — give up old behaviors, change our attitudes and thoughts to agree with His will. When we enable others to sin against us we become a partner in their sin and its penalties.

- Do not isolate yourself believing that no one else has ever suffered as you. The Word says that our sufferings are common to man. Attend a local church were you can receive godly counseling and guidance. Today, many churches have support groups where you will encounter those who understand your distress from personal experience. As they share the comfort they have received, you are comforted and encouraged.

- We pray with them asking God to give them the courage to take the action necessary to protect themselves and their children.

When everyone we have trusted betrays us, it is difficult to trust a God we cannot see. "Oh, for grace to trust Him more." Feelings of insecurity often control a woman's decisions to stay in an unhealthy, dangerous situation. One emotionally crippled woman shared that it was worth being abused to feel loved during peaceful times. She was able to walk away when she embraced the truth that Jesus loves me! Do not give up who you are created to be, or compromise your convictions to win the praise and approval of others.

Live truly, speak truly and deal truly in all the affairs of life. Make your ear attentive to skillful and godly Wisdom. Wisdom that comes from heaven is...wholehearted and straightforward and sincere. (James 3:17 LB) Walk in truth developing the fruit of the spirit, and follow the Holy Spirit in every area of your life. Choose your priorities. "Seek (aim at and strive after) first of all His kingdom and His righteousness (His way of doing and being right)...." (Matthew 6:33 AMP)

Hide God's Word in your heart. Know his teachings. They are true life and good health for you. Carefully guard your thoughts because they are the source of true life. Never tell lies or be deceitful in what you say. (Proverbs 2:2-4 CEV) When you maintain godly integrity, you will walk in righteousness, in love and in obedience to the Word of God.

Many women are controlled by the fear of never marrying, of being alone, of never having children — and the list goes on. Satan takes advantage of these fears and works his schemes to defeat and destroy women. Satan has hated women since Genesis 3:15. God said to him, "From now on you and the woman will be enemies, as will your offspring and hers. You will strike his heel, but he will crush your head." Jesus, our Savior, defeated him, stripped him of his power and authority. Today, we are the enforcers of the triumphant victory of our Lord Jesus Christ. It is time for each individual woman to arise, determine her worth and set high standards according to the will and purpose of God.

Unmarried women look at their married sisters, and cry, "You don't understand!" Many married women would gladly exchange their marriage problems for those of a single person. Some believe a woman is incomplete and made to feel "less than" worthy as a person without a mate. In some churches a single woman is never allowed to hold a leadership role because she is "unbalanced" without a spouse. How tragic that the church has forfeited its opportunity to train a powerful leader, and sacrificed valuable talents for man-made doctrines.

If singles and married women could have an open forum, both would discover that wholeness comes out of a personal relationship with Christ Jesus our Lord. You are complete in Him. More that one married woman has said, "I can't find myself. I don't know who I am. Why do I feel unfulfilled? What is wrong with me? I feel so fragmented." May times they blame the spouse. The chastisement needful to obtain our peace, emotional healing and well-being was upon Jesus. (Isaiah 53:5) When Jesus came and dwelt among us He revealed Jehovah as a loving Father. As you develop an intimate relationship with Him, you will learn to appreciate and to love yourself, and then, you can receive love and risk loving others.

You will find prayers to strengthen you whether you are single or married, a stay-at home Mother or a career person. Before beginning the day, prepare yourself by spending time in prayer and meditation. Yes, I am in ministry, and I love my work. Each day before I go to the office, I allow time to pray, meditate and read God's word and other helpful, inspiring materials for personal growth. When my children were home I had to rise early to have the necessary quiet time with my Father in prayer and Bible study. Jesus is made unto us wisdom, righteousness, sanctification and redemption. (1 Corinthians 1:30)

Prayer is conversation with our Heavenly Father. Take time to talk with Him and listen for His quiet, gentle voice. He knows your present circumstances and your future, and has already provided exactly what you need for the day. Collect your thoughts and prepare to take care of the daily activities. May God receive glory and honor as we go about our daily routines. I pray that others will come to know our Father Who is in heaven just because we have been in prayer with Jesus.

My prayer is that you will find strength, comfort, courage and fortitude as you pray according to God's Word. Grow in grace and the knowledge of our Lord and Savior Jesus Christ, ever learning, ever growing, and ever achieving. Faith comes by hearing, and hearing by the Word. When you hear yourself pray you will discover that you truly believe. God is a rewarder of those who believe that He is, and the He is a rewarder of those who diligently seek Him.

Oh, what manner of love has the Father bestowed upon you that He would call you His daughter! You are a daugher of the Most High God. He equips you to overcome obstacles and to succeed in every area of your life. YOU ARE GOD'S WOMAN!

Loving in Jesus' Name,
Germaine Copeland
Your Sister in Christ

Personal Confessions

Jesus is Lord over my spirit, my soul, and my body. (Phil. 2:9-11.)

Jesus has been made unto me wisdom, righteousness, sanctification, and redemption. I can do all things through Christ Who strengthens me. (1 Cor. 1:30, Phil. 4:13.)

The Lord is my shepherd. I do not want. My God supplies all my need according to His riches in glory in Christ Jesus. (Ps. 23, Phil. 4:19.)

I do not fret or have anxiety about anything. I do not have a care. (Phil. 4:6, 1 Pet. 5:6,7.)

I am the Body of Christ. I am redeemed from the curse, because Jesus bore my sicknesses and carried my diseases in His own body. By His stripes I am healed. I forbid any sickness or disease to operate in my body. Every organ, every tissue of my body functions in the perfection in which God created it to function. I honor God and bring glory to Him in my body. (Gal. 3:13, Matt. 8:17, 1 Pet. 2:24, 1 Cor. 6:20.)

I have the mind of Christ and hold the thoughts, feelings, and purposes of His heart. (1 Cor. 2:16.)

I am a believer and not a doubter. I hold fast to my confession of faith. I decide to walk by faith and practice faith. My faith comes by hearing and hearing by the Word of God. Jesus is the author and the developer of my faith. (Heb. 4:14, Heb. 11:6, Rom. l0:17, Heb. 12:2.)

21

The love of God has been shed abroad in my heart by the Holy Spirit and His love abides in me richly. I keep myself in the Kingdom of light, in love, in the Word, and the wicked one touches me not. (Rom. 5:5, 1 John 4:16, 1 John 5:18.)

I tread upon serpents and scorpions and over all the power of the enemy. I take my shield of faith and quench his every fiery dart. Greater is He Who is in me than he who is in the world. (Ps. 91:13, Eph. 6:16, 1 John 4:4.)

I am delivered from this present evil world. I am seated with Christ in heavenly places. I reside in the Kingdom of God's dear Son. The law of the Spirit of life in Christ Jesus has made me free from the law of sin and death. (Gal. 1:4, Eph. 2:6, Col. 1:13, Rom. 8:2.)

I fear *not* for God has given me a spirit of power, of love, and of a sound mind. God is on my side. (2 Tim. 1:7, Rom. 8:31.)

I hear the voice of the Good Shepherd. I hear my Father's voice, and the voice of a stranger I will not follow. I roll my works upon the Lord. I commit and trust them wholly to Him. He will cause my thoughts to become agreeable to His will, and so shall my plans be established and succeed. (John 10:27, Prov. 16:3.)

I am a world overcomer because I am born of God. I represent the Father and Jesus well. I am a useful member in the Body of Christ. I am His workmanship recreated in Christ Jesus. My Father God is all the while effectually at work in me both to will and do His good pleasure. (1 John 5:4,5, Eph. 2:10, Phil. 2:13.)

I let the Word dwell in me richly. He Who began a good work in me will continue until the day of Christ. (Col. 3:16, Phil. 1:6.)

Prayers for Personal Needs

One

To Receive Jesus as Savior and Lord

Father, it is written in Your Word that if I confess with my mouth that Jesus is Lord and believe in my heart that You have raised Him from the dead, I shall be saved. Therefore, Father, I confess that Jesus is my Lord. I make Him Lord of my life right now. I believe in my heart that You raised Jesus from the dead. I renounce my past life with Satan and close the door to any of his devices.

I thank You for forgiving me of all my sin. Jesus is my Lord, and I am a new creation. Old things have passed away. Now all things become new in Jesus' name. Amen.

27

Scripture References

John 3:16

John 6:37

John 10:10b

Romans 3:23

2 Corinthians 5:19

John 16:8,9

Romans 5:8

John 14:6

Romans 10:9,10

Romans 10:13

Ephesians 2:1-10

2 Corinthians 5:17

John 1:12

2 Corinthians 5:21

To Glorify God

In view of [all] the mercies of God, I make a decisive dedication of my body — presenting all my members and faculties — as a living sacrifice, holy (devoted, consecrated) and well pleasing to You, God, which is my reasonable (rational, intelligent) service and spiritual worship. It is [not in my own strength] for it is You, Lord, Who is all the while effectually at work in me — energizing and creating in me the power and desire — both to will and work for Your good pleasure and satisfaction and delight.

Father, I will not draw back or shrink in fear, for then Your soul would have no delight or pleasure in me. I was bought for a price — purchased with a preciousness and paid for, made Your very own. So, then, I honor You, Lord, and bring glory to You in my body.

I called on You in the day of trouble; You delivered me, and I shall honor and glorify you. I rejoice because You delivered me and drew me to Yourself out of the control and dominion of darkness *(obscurity)* and transferred me into the kingdom of the Son of Your love. I will confess and praise You, O Lord my God, with my whole (united) heart; and I will glorify Your name for evermore.

As a bond servant of Jesus Christ, I receive and develop the talents which have been given me, for I would have You say of me, "Well done, you upright (honorable, admirable) and faithful servant!" I make use of the gifts (faculties, talents, qualities) according to the grace given me. I let my light so shine before men that they may see my moral excellence and my praiseworthy, noble and good deeds, and recognize and honor and praise and glorify my Father Who is in heaven.

In the name of Jesus, I allow my life to lovingly express truth in all things — speaking truly, dealing truly, living truly. Whatever I do — no matter what it is — in word or deed, I do everything in the name of the Lord Jesus and in [dependence upon] His Person, giving praise to God the Father through Him. Whatever may be my task, I work at it heartily (from the soul), as [something done] for the Lord and not for men. To God the Father be all glory and honor and praise. Amen.

29

Scripture References (AMP)

Romans 12:1

Philippians 2:13

Hebrews 10:38b

1 Corinthians 6:20

Psalm 50:15

Colossians 1:13

Psalm 86:12

Matthew 25:21

Romans 12:6

Matthew 5:16

Ephesians 4:15

Colossians 3:17

Colossians 3:23

Three

Knowing God's Will

Father, in Jesus' name, I thank You that You are instructing me in the way which I should go and that You are guiding me with Your eye. I thank You for Your guidance and leading concerning Your will, Your plan, and Your purpose for my life. I do hear the voice of the Good Shepherd, for I know You and follow You. You lead me in the paths of righteousness for Your name's sake.

Thank You, Father, that my path is growing brighter and brighter until it reaches the full light of day. As I follow You, Lord, I believe my path is becoming clearer each day.

31

Thank You, Father, that Jesus was made unto me wisdom. Confusion is not a part of my life. I am not confused about Your will for my life. I trust in You and lean not unto my own understanding. As I acknowledge You in all my ways, You are directing my paths. I believe that as I trust in You completely, You will show me the path of life. Amen.

Scripture References

Psalm 32:8

John 10:3,4

Psalm 23:3

Proverbs 4:18

Ephesians 5:19

1 Corinthians 1:30

1 Corinthians 14:33

Proverbs 3:5,6

Psalm 16:11

Four

Godly Wisdom in the Affairs of Life

Father, You said if anyone lacks wisdom, let him ask of You, Who giveth to all men liberally, and upbraideth not; and it shall be given him. Therefore, I ask in faith, nothing wavering, to be filled with the knowledge of Your will in all wisdom and spiritual understanding. Today I incline my ear unto wisdom, and apply my heart to understanding so that I might receive that which has been freely given unto me.

In the name of Jesus, I receive skill and godly wisdom and instruction. I discern and comprehend the words of understanding and insight. I receive instruction in wise dealing and the discipline of wise thoughtfulness, righteousness, justice, and integrity. Prudence, knowledge, discretion, and discernment are given to me. I increase in knowledge. As a person of understanding, I acquire skill and attain to sound counsels [so that I may be able to steer my course rightly].

Wisdom will keep, defend, and protect me; I love her and she guards me. I prize Wisdom highly

33

and exalt her; she will bring me to honor because I embrace her. She gives to my head a wreath of gracefulness; a crown of beauty and glory will she deliver to me. Length of days is in her right hand, and in her left hand are riches and honor.

Jesus has been made unto me wisdom, and in Him are all the treasures of [divine] wisdom, [of comprehensive insight into the ways and purposes of God], and [all the riches of spiritual] knowledge and enlightenment are stored up and lie hidden. God has hidden away sound and godly wisdom and stored it up for me, for I am the righteousness of God in Christ Jesus.

Therefore, I will walk in paths of uprightness. When I walk, my steps shall not be hampered — my path will be clear and open; and when I run I shall not stumble. I take fast hold of instruction, and do not let her go; I guard her, for she is my life. I let my eyes look right on [with fixed purpose], and my gaze is straight before me. I consider well the path of my feet, and I let all my ways be established and ordered aright.

Father, in the name of Jesus, I look carefully to how I walk! I live purposefully and worthily and accurately, not as unwise and witless, but as a wise — sensible, intelligent person; making the very most of my time — buying up every opportunity. Amen.

34

Scripture References

James 1:5,6a

Colossians 1:9b

Proverbs 2:2

Proverbs 1:2-5 AMP

Proverbs 4:6,8,9 AMP

Proverbs 3:16 AMP

1 Corinthians 1:30

Colossians 2:3 AMP

Proverbs 2:7 AMP

2 Corinthians 5:21

Proverbs 4:11-13,25,26 AMP

Ephesians 5:15,16 AMP

Five

Conquering the Thought Life

In the name of Jesus, I take authority over my thought life. Even though I walk (live) in the flesh, I am not carrying on my warfare according to the flesh and using mere human weapons. For the weapons of my warfare are not physical (weapons of flesh and blood), but they are mighty before God for the overthrow and destruction of strongholds. I refute arguments and theories and reasonings and every proud and lofty thing that sets itself up against the (true) knowledge of God; and I lead every thought and purpose away captive into the obedience of Christ, the Messiah, the Anointed One.

With my soul I will bless the Lord with every thought and purpose in life. My mind will not wander out of the presence of God. My life shall glorify the Father — *spirit, soul, and body*. I take no account of the evil done to me — I pay no attention to a suffered wrong. It holds no place in my thought life. I am ever ready to believe the best of every person. I gird up the loins of my mind, and I set my mind and keep it set on what is above

— the higher things — not on the things that are on the earth.

Whatever is true, whatever is worthy of reverence and is honorable and seemly, whatever is just, whatever is pure, whatever is lovely and lovable, whatever is kind and winsome and gracious, if there is any virtue and excellence, if there is anything worthy of praise, I will think on and weigh and take account of these things — I will fix my mind on them.

The carnal mind is no longer operative for I have the mind of Christ, the Messiah, and do hold the thoughts (feelings and purposes) of His heart. In the name of Jesus, I will practice what I have learned and received and heard and seen in Christ, and model my way of living on it, and the God of peace — of untroubled, undisturbed well-being — will be with me.

37

In Jesus' name, amen.

Scripture References (AMP)

2 Corinthians 10:3-5   Colossians 3:2

Psalm 103:1   Philippians 4:8

1 Corinthians 6:20   1 Corinthians 2:16

1 Corinthians 13:5b,7a   Philippians 4:9

1 Peter 1:13

∽ Six ∽

Walking in Humility

Father, I clothe myself with humility [as the garb of a servant, so that its covering cannot possibly be stripped from me]. I renounce pride and arrogance. Father, You give grace to the humble. Therefore I humble myself under Your mighty hand, that in due time You may exalt me.

In the name of Jesus, I cast the whole of my care [all my anxieties, all my worries, all my concerns for my future, once and for all] on You, for You care for me affectionately and care about me watchfully. I expect a life of victory and awesome deeds because my actions are done on behalf of a spirit humbly submitted to Your truth and righteousness.

Father, in the name of Jesus, I refuse to be wise in my own eyes; but I choose to fear You and shun evil. This will bring health to my body and nourishment to my bones.

Father, I humble myself and submit to Your Word that speaks...exposes, sifts, analyzes, and judges the very thoughts and purposes of my heart. I test my own actions, so that I might have appropriate self-esteem, without comparing myself to anyone else. The security of Your guidance will allow me to carry my own load with energy and confidence.

I listen carefully and hear what is being said to me. I incline my ear to wisdom and apply my heart to understanding and insight. Humility and fear of You bring wealth and honor and life.

Father, I hide Your Word in my heart that I might not sin against You. As one of Your chosen people, holy and dearly loved, I clothe myself with compassion, kindness, humility, gentleness, and patience. I bear with others and forgive whatever grievances I may have against anyone. I forgive as You forgave me. And over all these virtues I put on love, which binds them all together in perfect unity. I let the peace of Christ rule in my heart, and I am thankful for Your grace and the power of the Holy Spirit.

Father, may Your will be done on earth in my life as it is in heaven.

In Jesus' name, amen.

39

Scripture References

1 Peter 5:5-7 *AMP*
Proverbs 3:7,8 *NIV*
Hebrews 4:12 *AMP*
Galatians 6:4,5 *NIV*
Proverbs 2:2 *NIV*

Proverbs 22:4 *NIV*
Psalm 119:11
Colossians 3:12-15 *NIV*
Matthew 6:10 *NIV*

∽ Seven ∾

To Watch What You Say

Father, today, I make a commitment to You in the name of Jesus. I turn from idle words and foolishly talking things that are contrary to my true desire to myself and toward others. Your Word says that the tongue defiles; that the tongue sets on fire the course of nature; that the tongue is set on fire of hell.

In the name of Jesus, I am determined to take control of my tongue. I am determined that hell will not set my tongue on fire. I renounce, reject, and repent of every word that has ever proceeded out of my mouth against You, God, and Your operation. I cancel its power and dedicate my mouth to speak excellent and right things. My mouth shall utter truth.

I am the righteousness of God. I set the course of my life for obedience, for abundance, for wisdom, for health, and for joy. Everything I speak is becoming to God. I refuse to compromise or err from pure and sound words. The words of my mouth and my deeds shall show forth Your righteousness and Your

40

salvation all of my days. I guard my mouth and my heart with all diligence. I refuse to give Satan any place in me.

Father, Your Words are top priority to me. They are spirit and life. I let the Word dwell in me richly in all wisdom. The ability of God is released within me by the words of my mouth and by the Word of God. I speak Your Words out of my mouth. They are alive in me. You are alive and working in me. So, I can boldly say that my words are words of faith, words of power, words of love, and words of life. They produce good things in my life and in the lives of others. Because I choose Your Words for my lips, I choose Your will for my life, and I go forth in the power of those words to perform them in Jesus' name. Amen.

Scripture References

Ephesians 5:4

2 Timothy 2:16

James 3:6

Proverbs 8:6,7

2 Corinthians 5:21

Proverbs 4:23

Proverbs 21:23

Ephesians 4:27

James 1:6

John 6:63

Colossians 3:16

Philemon 6

∽ Eight ∾

To Live Free From Worry

Father, I thank You that I have been delivered from the power of darkness and translated into the Kingdom of Your dear Son. *I commit to live free from worry in the name of Jesus,* for the law of the Spirit of life in Christ Jesus has made me *free* from the law of sin and death.

I humble myself under Your mighty hand that in due time You may exalt me. I cast the whole of my cares *(name them)* — all my anxieties, all my worries, all my concerns, once and for all — on You. You care for me affectionately and care about me watchfully. You sustain me. You will never allow the consistently righteous to be moved — made to slip, fall, or fail!

Father, I delight myself in You, and You perfect that which concerns me.

I cast down imaginations (reasonings) and every high thing that exalts itself against the knowledge of You, and bring into captivity every thought to the obedience of Christ. I lay aside every weight and the sin of worry which does try so easily to beset me. I run with patience the race that is set before me, looking unto Jesus, the author and finisher of my faith.

I thank You, Father, that You are able to keep that which I have committed unto You. I think on (fix my mind on) those things that are true, honest, just, pure, lovely, of good report, virtuous, and deserving of praise. I let not my heart be troubled. I abide in Your Words, and Your Words abide in me. Therefore, Father, I do *not* forget what manner of person I am. I look into the perfect law of liberty and continue therein, being *not* a forgetful hearer, but a *doer of the Word* and thus blessed in my doing!

Thank You, Father. *I am carefree.* I walk in that peace which passes all understanding in Jesus' name! Amen.

43

Scripture References

Colossians 1:13	Hebrews 12:1,2
Romans 8:2	2 Timothy 1:12
1 Peter 5:6,7 AMP	Philippians 4:8
Psalm 55:22	John 14:1
Psalm 138:8	James 1:22-25
2 Corinthians 10:5	Philippians 4:6

∽ Nine ∾

Pleading the Blood of Jesus

I.

Morning Prayer [1]

Father, I come in the name of Jesus to plead His blood on my life and on all that belongs to me, and on all that over which You have made me a steward.

I plead the blood of Jesus on the portals of my mind, my body (the temple of the Holy Spirit), my emotions, and my will. I believe that I am protected by the blood of the Lamb that gives me access to the Holy of Holies.

I plead the blood on my children, my grandchildren, and their children, and on all those whom You have given me in this life.

Lord, You have said that the life of the flesh is in the blood. Thank You for this blood that has cleansed me from sin, and sealed the New Covenant of which I am a partaker.

In Jesus' name, amen.

---

[1] Based on a prayer written by Joyce Meyer in *The Word, the Name and the Blood* (Tulsa: Harrison House, 1995).

Scripture References

Exodus 12:7,13   Leviticus 17:11

1 Corinthians 6:19   1 John 1:7

Hebrews 9:6-14   Hebrews 13:20 AMP

II.

Evening Prayer[2]

Father, as I lie down to sleep, I plead the blood of Jesus upon my life — within me, around me, and between me and all evil and the author of evil.

In Jesus' name, amen.

---

[2] Based on a prayer written by Mrs. C. Nuzum as recorded by Billye Brim in *The Blood and The Glory* (Tulsa: Harrison House, 1995).

45

∽ Ten ∽

Breaking the Curse of Abuse

Introduction

Christ redeemed us from the curse of the law by becoming a curse for us, for it is written: "Cursed is everyone who is hung on a tree."

Galatians 3:13 NIV

46

On a Sunday morning after I had taught a lesson titled "Healing for the Emotionally Wounded," a young man wanted to speak with me. I listened intently as he told me that he had just been released from jail and was now on probation for physically abusing his family. His wife had filed for divorce, and he was living alone. It was not easy for him to confess his sin to me, and I was impressed by his humble attitude.

He said, "I am glad that this message is being given in the Church, and the abused can receive ministry. Is there anywhere that the abuser can go to receive spiritual help?"

He shared with me that he was attending a support group for abusers. He desired to commit to a church where he could receive forgiveness and acceptance. He knew that any lasting change would have to be from the inside out by the Spirit. I prayed with him, but it would be three years before I could write a prayer for the abuser.

As I read, studied, and sought the Lord, I discovered that the abuser is usually a person who has been abused. Often, the problem is a generational curse that has been in the family of the abuser for as far back as anyone can remember. Many times the abuser declares that he will never treat his wife and children as he has been treated, but in spite of his resolve he finds himself reacting in the same violent manner.

47

The generational curse is reversed as the abuser is willing to allow God to remove the character flaws that have held him in bondage.

If you are an abuser, I encourage you to pray this prayer for yourself until it becomes a reality in your life. If you know someone who is an abuser, pray this as a prayer of intercession in the third person.

Prayer

I receive and confess that Jesus is my Lord, and I ask that Your will be done in my life.

Father, You have rescued me from the dominion of darkness and have brought me into the Kingdom of the Son of Your love. Once I was darkness, but now I am light in You; I walk as a child of light. The abuse is exposed and reproved by the light, it is made visible and clear; and where everything is visible and clear there is light.

Help me to grow in grace (undeserved favor, spiritual strength) and recognition and knowledge and understanding of my Lord and Savior, Jesus Christ, so that I may experience Your love and trust You to be a Father to me.

The history of my earthly family is filled with abusive behavior, much hatred, strife, and rage. The painful memory of past abuse *(verbal, emotional, physical, and/or sexual)* has caused me to be hostile and abusive to others.

I desire to be a doer of the Word, and not a hearer only. No matter which way I turn, I can't make myself do right. I want to, but I can't. When I want to do good, I don't; and when I try not to do wrong, I do it anyway. It seems that sin still has me in its evil grasp. This pain has caused me to hurt myself and

48

others. In my mind I want to be Your willing servant, but instead I find myself still enslaved to sin.

I confess my sin of abuse, resentment, and hostility toward others, and I ask You to forgive me. You are faithful and just to forgive my sin and cleanse me from all unrighteousness. I am tired of reliving the past in my present life, perpetuating the generational curse of anger and abuse.

Jesus was made a curse for me; therefore, Lord, I put on Your whole armor that I may be able to successfully stand against all the strategies and the tricks of the devil. I thank You that the evil power of abuse is broken, overthrown, and cast down. I submit myself to You and resist the devil. The need to hurt others no longer controls me or my family.

In Jesus' name, amen.

49

Scripture References

Romans 10:9

Matthew 6:10

Colossians 1:13 AMP

Ephesians 5:8,13 AMP

2 Peter 3:18 AMP

James 1:22

Romans 7:18-25 TLB

1 John 1:9

Galatians 3:13

Ephesians 6:11,12 TLB

2 Corinthians 10:5

James 4:7

∽ Eleven ∾

Healing From Abuse

Introduction

This prayer can be applied to any form of abuse — physical, mental, emotional, or sexual. I wrote it after reading T. D. Jakes' book, *Woman, Thou Art Loosed*.[4] By praying it, I personally have experienced victory and freedom — I am no longer a victim but an overcomer.

Prayer

Lord, You are my High Priest, and I ask You to loose me from this "infirmity." The abuse I suffered pronounced me guilty and condemned. I was bound — in an emotional prison — crippled, and could in no wise lift up myself. You have called me to Yourself, and I have come.

The anointing that is upon You is present to bind up and heal the brokenness and emotional wounds of the past. You are the Truth that makes me free.

---

[1] (Shippensburg, PA: Treasure House, 1993).

Thank You, Lord, for guiding me through the steps to emotional wholeness. You have begun a good work in me, and You will perform it until the day of Christ Jesus.

Father, I desire to live according to the Spirit of life in Christ Jesus. This Spirit of life in Christ, like a strong wind, has magnificently cleared the air, freeing me from a fated lifetime of brutal tyranny at the hands of abuse.

Since I am now free, it is my desire to forget those things that lie behind and strain forward to what lies ahead. I press on toward the goal to win the [supreme and heavenly] prize to which You in Christ Jesus are calling me upward. The past will no longer control my thinking patterns or my behavior.

Praise be to You! I am a new creature in Christ Jesus. Old things have passed away; and, behold, all things have become new. I declare and decree that henceforth I will walk in newness of life.

51

Forgive me, Father, for self-hatred and self-condemnation. I am Your child. You sent Jesus that I might have life and have it more abundantly. Thank You for the blood of Jesus that makes me whole.

It is my desire to throw all spoiled virtue and cancerous evil in the garbage. In simple humility, I let my Gardener, You Lord, landscape me with the Word, making a salvation-garden of my life.

Father, by Your grace, I forgive my abuser/abusers and ask You to bring him/her/them to repentance.

In the name of Jesus I pray, amen.

Scripture References

Luke 13:11,12	Romans 6:4
John 14:6	1 John 3:1,2
John 8:32	John 10:10
Philippians 1:6	1 John 1:7
Romans 8:2 MESSAGE	James 1:21 MESSAGE
Philippians 3:13,14 AMP	Matthew 5:44
2 Corinthians 5:17	2 Peter 3:9

∽ Twelve ∾

Letting Go of the Past

Father, I realize my helplessness in saving myself, and I glory in what Christ Jesus has done for me. I let go — put aside all past sources of my confidence — counting them worth less than nothing, in order that I may experience Christ and become one with Him.

Lord, I have received Your Son, and He has given me the authority (power, privilege, and right) to become Your child.

I unfold my past and put into proper perspective those things that are behind. I have been crucified with Christ, and I no longer live, but Christ lives in me. The life I live in the body, I live by faith in the Son of God, Who loved me and gave Himself for me. I trust in You, Lord, with all my heart and lean not on my own understanding. In all my ways I acknowledge You, and You will make my paths straight.

I want to know Christ and the power of His resurrection and the fellowship of sharing in His sufferings, becoming like Him in His death, and so, somehow, to attain to the resurrection from the dead. So, whatever it takes, I will be one who lives

53

in the fresh newness of life of those who are alive from the dead.

I don't mean to say that I am perfect. I haven't learned all I should even yet, but I keep working toward that day when I will finally be all that Christ saved me for and wants me to be.

I am bringing all my energies to bear on this one thing: regardless of my past I look forward to what lies ahead. I strain to reach the end of the race and receive the prize for which You are calling me up to heaven because of what Christ Jesus did for me.

In His name I pray, amen.

Scripture References

Philippians 3:7-9 TLB

John 1:12 AMP

Psalm 32:5 AMP

Philippians 3:13

Galatians 2:20 NIV

Proverbs 3:5,6 NIV

Philippians 3:10,11 NIV

Romans 6:4

Philippians 3:12-14 TLB

✍ *Thirteen* ✍

Strength to Overcome Cares and Burdens

Why are you cast down, O my inner self? And why should you moan over me and be disquieted within me?

Father, You set Yourself against the proud and haughty, but give grace [continually] unto the humble. I submit myself therefore to You, God. In the name of Jesus, I resist the devil, and he will flee from me. I resist the cares of the world which try to pressure me daily. Except the Lord builds the house, they labor in vain who build it.

55

Jesus, I come to You, for I labor and am heavy laden and over burdened, and You cause me to rest — You will ease and relieve and refresh my soul.

I take Your Yoke upon me, and I learn of You; for You are gentle (meek) and humble (lowly) in heart, and I will find rest — relief, ease and refreshment and recreation and blessed quiet — for my soul. For Your yoke is wholesome *(easy)* — not harsh, hard, sharp or pressing, but comfortable, gracious and pleasant; and Your burden is light and easy to be borne.

I cast my burden on You, Lord, [releasing the weight of it] and You will sustain me; I thank You that You will never allow me, the [consistently] righteous, to be moved — made to slip, fall or fail.

In the name of Jesus, I withstand the devil. I am firm in my faith [against his onset] — rooted, established, strong, immovable and determined. I cease from [the weariness and pain] of human labor; and am zealous and exert myself and strive diligently to enter into the rest [of God] — to know and experience it for myself.

Father, I thank You that Your presence goes with me, and that You give me rest. I am still and rest in You, Lord; I wait for You, and patiently stay myself upon You. I will not fret myself, nor shall I let my heart be troubled, neither shall I let it be afraid. I hope in You, God, and wait expectantly for You; for I shall yet praise You, for You are the help of my countenance, and my God.

In Jesus' name, amen.

Scripture References (AMP)

Psalm 42:11a

James 4:6,7

Psalm 127:1a

Matthew 11:28-30

Psalm 55:22

1 Peter 5:9a

Hebrews 4:10b,11

Exodus 33:14

Psalm 37:7

John 14:27b

Psalm 42:11b

↠ Fourteen ↞

Healing for Damaged Emotions

Father, in the name of Jesus, I come to You with a feeling of shame and emotional hurt. I confess my transgressions to You [continually unfolding the past till all is told]. You are faithful and just to forgive me and cleanse me of all unrighteousness. You are my hiding place and You, Lord, preserve me from trouble. You surround me with songs and shouts of deliverance. I have chosen life and according to Your Word You saw me while I was being formed in my mother's womb and on the authority of Your Word I was wonderfully made. Now, I am Your handiwork, recreated in Christ Jesus.

Father, You have delivered me from the spirit of fear and I shall not be ashamed. Neither shall I be confounded and depressed. You gave me beauty for ashes, the oil of joy for mourning and the garment of praise for the spirit of heaviness that I might be a tree of righteousness, the planting of the Lord, that You might be glorified. I speak out in psalms, hymns and spiritual songs, offering praise with my voice

57

and making melody with all my heart to the Lord. Just as David did in 1 Samuel 30:6 I encourage myself in the Lord.

I believe in God Who raised Jesus from the dead, Who was betrayed and put to death because of my misdeeds and was raised to secure my acquittal, absolving me from all guilt before God. Father, You anointed Jesus and sent Him to bind up and heal my broken heart, and liberate me from the shame of my youth and the imperfections of my caretakers. In the name of Jesus, I choose to forgive all those who have wronged me in any way. You will not leave me without support as I complete the forgiveness process. I take comfort and am encouraged and confidently say, "The Lord is my Helper; I will not be seized with alarm. What can man do to me?"

My spirit is the candle of the Lord searching all the innermost parts of my being and the Holy Spirit leads me into all truth. When reality exposes shame and emotional pain, I remember that the sufferings of this present life are not worth being compared with the glory that is about to be revealed to me and in me and for me and conferred on me! The chastisement needful to obtain my peace and well-being was upon Jesus, and with the stripes that wounded Him I was healed and made whole. As Your child,

Father, I have a joyful and confident hope of eternal salvation. This hope will never disappoint, delude or shame me, for God's love has been poured out in my heart through the Holy Spirit Who has been given to me.

In His name I pray, amen.

Scripture References

Psalm 32:5-7 AMP

1 John 1:9

Deuteronomy 30:19

Psalm 139

Ephesians 2:10

2 Timothy 1:7

Isaiah 54:4

Isaiah 61:3

Ephesians 5:19

Romans 4:24,25

Isaiah 61:1

Mark 11:25

Hebrews 13:5,6

Proverbs 20:27

John 16:13

Romans 8:18

Isaiah 53:5b

Romans 5:3-5

59

∼ Fifteen ∼

Victory Over Pride

Father, Your Word says that You hate a proud look, that You resist the proud but give grace to the humble. I submit myself therefore to You, God. In the name of Jesus, I resist the devil, and he will flee from me. I renounce every manifestation of pride in my life as sin; I repent and turn from it.

As an act of faith, I clothe myself with humility and receive Your grace. I humble myself under Your mighty hand, Lord, that You may exalt me in due time. I refuse to exalt myself. I do not think of myself more highly than I ought; I do not have an exaggerated opinion of my own importance, but rate my ability with sober judgment, according to the degree of faith apportioned to me.

Proverbs 11:2 says, **When pride cometh, then cometh shame: but with the lowly is wisdom.** Father, I set myself to resist pride when it comes. My desire is to be counted among the lowly, so I take on the attitude of a servant.

Father, thank You that You dwell with him who is of a contrite and humble spirit. You revive the spirit of the humble and revive the heart of the contrite ones. Thank You that the reward of humility and the reverent and worshipful fear of the Lord is riches and honor and life.

In Jesus' name I pray, amen.

Scripture References

Proverbs 6:16

James 4:6,7

Proverbs 21:4

1 Peter 5:5,6

Romans 12:3 AMP

Proverbs 11:2

Matthew 23:11

Isaiah 57:15

Proverbs 22:4 AMP

Sixteen

Victory Over Gluttony

Father, it is written in Your Word that if I confess with my lips that Jesus is Lord and believe in my heart that You have raised Him from the dead, I shall be saved. Father, I am Your child and confess that Jesus Christ is Lord over my spirit, my soul, and my body. I make Him Lord over every situation in my life. Therefore, I can do all things through Christ Jesus Who strengthens me.

Father, *I have made a quality decision to give You my appetite*. I choose *Jesus* rather than the indulgence of my flesh. I command my body to get in line with Your Word. I eat only as much as is sufficient for me. I eat and am satisfied.

When I sit down to eat, I consider what is before me. I am not given to the desire of dainties or deceitful foods.

Like a boxer, I buffet my body — handle it roughly, discipline it by hardships — and subdue it. I bring my body into subjection to my spirit man — the inward man — the real me. Not all things are helpful — good for me to do though permissible. I will not become the slave of anything or be brought under its power.

My body is for the Lord. I dedicate my body presenting all my members and faculties — as a living sacrifice, holy and well pleasing to You, presenting them as implements of righteousness. I am united to You, Lord, and become one spirit with You. My body is the temple, the very sanctuary, of the Holy Spirit Who lives within me, Whom I have received as a gift from You, Father.

I am not my own. I was bought for a price, made Your own. So then, I honor You and bring glory to You in my body. Therefore, I always exercise and discipline myself, bringing under authority my carnal affections, bodily appetites, and worldly desires. I endeavor in all respects to have a clean conscience, void of offense toward You, Father, and toward men. I keep myself from idols — from anything and everything that would occupy the place in my heart due to You, from any sort of substitute for You that would take first place in my life.

63

I no longer spend the rest of my natural life living by my human appetites and desires, but I live for what You will! I am on my guard. I refuse to be overburdened and depressed, weighed down with the giddiness and headache and nausea of self-indulgence, drunkenness (on food), worldly worries and cares, for I have been given a spirit of power and of love and of a sound mind. I have discipline and self-control.

Father, I *do* resist temptation in the name of Jesus. I strip off and throw aside every encumbrance — unnecessary weight — and this gluttony which so readily tries to cling to and entangle me. I run with patient endurance and steady persistence the appointed course of the race that is set before me, looking away from all distractions to Jesus, the author and finisher of my faith.

Christ the Messiah *will* be magnified and get glory and praise in this body of mine and *will* be boldly exalted in my person. Thank You, Father, in Jesus' name! Hallelujah! Amen.

64

Scripture References

Romans 10:9,10	Romans 6:13
Philippians 4:13	1 Corinthians 9:27 AMP
Deuteronomy 30:19	1 Corinthians 6:19,20 AMP
Romans 13:14	Romans 12:1 AMP
Proverbs 25:16	Luke 21:34 AMP
2 Timothy 1:7 AMP	1 Corinthians 6:12,13,17 AMP
Proverbs 23:1-3	James 4:7
Hebrews 12:1,2 AMP	Philippians 1:20 AMP

∽ Seventeen ∾

Victory Over Fear

Father, in Jesus' name, I confess and believe that no weapon formed against me shall prosper, and any tongue that rises against me in judgment I shall show to be in the wrong. I believe I dwell in the secret place of the Most High. I shall remain stable and fixed under the shadow of the Almighty God whose power no foe can withstand — this secret place hides me from the strife of tongues.

I believe the wisdom of God's Word dwells in me, and because it does, I realize that I am without fear or dread of evil. In all my ways I know and acknowledge God and His Word; thus, He directs and makes straight and plain my pathway. As I attend to God's Word, it is health to my nerves and sinews, and marrow and moistening to my bones.

I am strengthened and reinforced with mighty power in my inner self by the Holy Spirit Himself Who dwells in me. God is my strength and my refuge, and I confidently trust in Him and in His Word. I am empowered through my union with Almighty God.

This gives me the superhuman, supernatural strength to walk in divine health and to live in abundance.

God Himself has said, **I will never leave you without support or forsake you or let you down, my child. [I will] not, [I will] not, [I will] not in any degree leave you helpless or relax my hold on you...assuredly not!** (Based on Hebrews 13:5 AMP.)

I take comfort and am encouraged and confidently and boldly say, "The Lord is my helper. I will not be seized with alarm. I will not fear or be terrified, for what can man do to me?"

I confess and believe that my children are disciples taught of the Lord and obedient to God's will. Great is the peace and undisturbed composure of my children — because God Himself contends with those who contend with me and my children, and He gives my children safety and eases them. God will perfect that which concerns me.

This Word of God that I have spoken is alive and full of power. It is active and operative. It energizes me, and it affects me. As I speak God's Word, it is sharper than any two-edged sword, and it is penetrating into my joints and into the marrow of my bones. It is healing to my flesh. It is prosperity for me. It is the magnificent Word of Almighty God. According to His Word that I have spoken, so be it! Hallelujah! Amen.

Scripture References

Isaiah 54:17 AMP

Psalm 91:1 AMP

Psalm 31:20

Proverbs 3:6,8 AMP

Ephesians 3:16 AMP

Psalm 91:2

Ephesians 6:10 AMP

Hebrews 13:5,6 AMP

Isaiah 54:13 AMP

Isaiah 49:25 AMP

Psalm 138:8 AMP

Hebrews 4:12 AMP

Eighteen

Overcoming Discouragement

Introduction

Moses returned to the Lord and said, "O Lord, why have you brought trouble upon this people? Is this why you sent me? Ever since I went to Pharaoh to speak in your name, he has brought trouble upon this people, and you have not rescued your people at all."

Exodus 5:22,23 NIV

68

Here in this passage, we find Moses discouraged, complaining to God.

It is important that we approach God with integrity in an attitude of humility. Because we fear making a negative confession, we sometimes cross the line of honesty into the line of denial and delusion.

Let's be honest. God already knows what we are feeling. He can handle our anger, complaints, and disappointments. He understands us. He is aware of our human frailties (Ps. 103:14) and can be touched with the feelings of our infirmities. (Heb. 4:15.)

Whether your "trouble" is a business failure, abandonment, depression, mental disorder, chemical imbalance, oppression, a marriage problem, a child who is in a strange land of drugs and alcohol, financial disaster, or anything else, the following prayer is for you.

Sometimes when you are in the midst of discouragement it is difficult to remember that you have ever known any Scripture. I admonish you to read this prayer aloud until you recognize the reality of God's Word in your spirit, soul, and body. Remember, God is watching over His Word to perform it. (Jer. 1:12 AMP.) He will perfect that which concerns you. (Ps. 138:8.)

Prayer

Lord, I have exhausted all my possibilities for changing my situation and circumstances and have found that I am powerless to change. I believe; help me overcome my unbelief. All things are not possible with man, but all things are possible with You. I humble myself before You, and You will lift me up.

I have a great High Priest Who has gone through the heavens, Jesus Your Son, and I hold firmly to the faith I profess. My High Priest is able to sympathize with my weaknesses. He was tempted in every way, just as I am — yet was without sin. I approach Your throne of grace with confidence,

69

so that I may receive mercy and find grace to help me in my time of need.

In the face of discouragement, disappointment, and anger, I choose to believe that Your word to Moses is Your word to me. You are mighty to deliver. Because of Your mighty hand, You will drive out the forces that have set themselves up against me. You are the Lord, Yahweh, the Promise-Keeper, the Almighty One. You appeared to Abraham, to Isaac, and to Jacob and established Your covenant with them.

Father, I believe that You have heard my groaning, my cries. I will live to see Your promises of deliverance fulfilled in my life. You have not forgotten one word of Your promise; You are a Covenant-Keeper.

It is You Who will bring me out from under the yoke of bondage and free me from being a slave to _____. You have redeemed me with an outstretched arm and with mighty acts of judgment. You have taken me as Your own, and You are my God. You are a Father to me. You have delivered me from the past that has held me in bondage and translated me into the Kingdom of love, peace, joy, and righteousness. I will no longer settle for the pain of the past. Where sin abounds, grace does much more abound.

Father, what You have promised, I will go and possess, in the name of Jesus. I am willing to take the chance, to take the risk, to get back into the good fight of faith. It is with patient endurance and steady and active persistence that I run the race, the appointed course that is set before me. I rebuke the spirit of fear for I am established in righteousness. Oppression and destruction shall not come near me. Behold, they may gather together and stir up strife, but it is not from You, Father. Whoever stirs up strife against me shall fall and surrender to me. I am more than a conqueror through Him Who loves me.

In His name I pray, amen.

Scripture References
(This prayer is based on Exodus 5:22-6:11 and includes other verses where applicable.)

Mark 9:24 NIV

Luke 18:27

1 Peter 5:6 NIV

Hebrews 4:14-16 NIV

Exodus 6:3,4 AMP

Genesis 49:22-26 AMP

1 Kings 8:56

Deuteronomy 26:8

Colossians 1:13

Romans 5:20

1 Timothy 6:12

Hebrews 12:1 AMP

Isaiah 54:14-16

Romans 8:37

71

ᴄᴏ *Nineteen* ᴄᴏ

Overcoming Intimidation

Father, I come to You in the name of Jesus, confessing that intimidation has caused me to stumble. I ask Your forgiveness for thinking of myself as inferior, for I am created in Your image, and I am Your workmanship. Jesus said that the Kingdom of God is in me. Therefore, the power that raised Jesus from the dead dwells in me and causes me to face life with hope and divine energy.

The Lord is my light and my salvation; whom shall I fear? The Lord is the strength of my life; of whom shall I be afraid? Lord, You said that You would never leave me or forsake me. Therefore, I can say without any doubt or fear that You are my helper, and I am not afraid of anything that mere man can do to me. Greater is He Who is in me than he who is in the world. If God is for me, who can be against me? I am free from the fear of man and public opinion.

Father, You have not given me a spirit of timidity — of cowardice, of craven and cringing and fawning fear — but You have given me a spirit of power and of love and of a calm and well-balanced mind and discipline and self-control. I can do all things through Christ Who gives me the strength. Amen.

Scripture References

1 John 1:9	Ephesians 2:10
Luke 17:21	Ephesians 1:19,20
Colossians 1:29	Psalm 1:27
Hebrews 13:5	1 John 4:4
Romans 3:31	Proverbs 29:25
2 Timothy 1:7	Philippians 4:13

73

~ Twenty ~

Overcoming a Sense of Hopelessness

Father, as Your child I boldly come before Your throne of grace that I may receive mercy and find grace to help in this time of need.

Father, I know that Your ears are open to my prayers. I ask that You listen to my prayer, O God, and hide not Yourself from my supplication!

I am calling upon You, my God, to rescue me. You redeem my life in peace from the battle of hopelessness that is against me. I cast my burden on You, Lord, [releasing the weight of it] and You sustain me; You will never allow the [consistently] righteous to be moved (made to slip, fall, or fail).

What time I am afraid, I will have confidence in and put my trust and reliance in You. By [Your help], God, I will praise Your Word; on You I lean, rely, and confidently put my trust; I will not fear.

You know my every sleepless night. Each tear and heartache is answered with Your promise. I am thanking You with all my heart. You pulled me from the brink of death, my feet from the cliff-edge of doom.

[What would have become of me], Lord, had I not believed that I would see Your goodness in the land of the living! I wait and hope for and expect You; I am brave and of good courage, and I let my heart be stout and enduring. Yes, I wait for and hope for and expect You.

Father, I give You all my worries and cares, for You are always thinking about me and watching everything that concerns me. I am well balanced and careful — vigilant, watching out for attacks from Satan, my great enemy. By Your grace I am standing firm, trusting You, and I remember that other Christians all around the world are going through these sufferings too. You, God, are full of kindness through Christ and will give me Your eternal glory.

75

In the name of Jesus I am an overcomer by the blood of the Lamb, and by the word of my testimony. Amen.

Scripture References

Hebrews 4:16

Psalm 55:1 MESSAGE

Psalm 55:1 AMP

Psalm 55:5 AMP

Psalm 55:16,18,22 AMP

Psalm 56:2,4 AMP

Psalm 56:5,8 MESSAGE

Psalm 56:13 MESSAGE

Psalm 27:13,14 AMP

1 Peter 5:7-9 AMP, TLB

Revelation 12:11

Twenty-One

Letting Go of Bitterness

Introduction

In interviews with divorced men and women, I have been encouraged to write a prayer on overcoming bitterness.

Often, the injustice of the situation in which these people find themselves creates deep hurts, wounds in the spirit, and anger that is so near the surface the individuals involved risk sinking into the trap of bitterness and revenge. Their thoughts may turn inward as they consider the unfairness of the situation and dwell on how badly they have been treated.

In a family divorce situation, bitterness sometimes distorts ideas of what is best for the child/children involved. One parent (and sometimes both parents) will use the child/children against the other.

Unresolved anger often moves one marriage partner to hurt the one he or she holds responsible for the hurt and sense of betrayal which they feel.

There is healing available. There is a way of escape for all who will turn to the Healer, obeying Him and trusting Him.

Prayer

Father, life seems so unjust, so unfair. The pain of rejection is almost more than I can bear. My past relationships have ended in strife, anger, rejection, and separation.

Lord, help me to let go of all bitterness and indignation and wrath (passion, rage, bad temper) and resentment (anger, animosity).

You are the One Who binds up and heals the brokenhearted. I receive Your anointing that destroys every yoke of bondage. I receive emotional healing by faith, and I thank You for giving me the grace to stand firm until the process is complete.

Thank You for wise counselors. I acknowledge the Holy Spirit as my wonderful Counselor. Thank You for helping me work out my salvation with fear and trembling, for it is You, Father, Who work in me to will and to act according to Your good purpose.

In the name of Jesus, I choose to forgive those who have wronged me. I purpose to live a life of forgiveness because You have forgiven me. With the help of the Holy Spirit, I get rid of all bitterness,

77

rage, and anger, brawling and slander, along with every form of malice. I desire to be kind and compassionate to others, forgiving them, just as in Christ You forgave me.

With the help of the Holy Spirit, I make every effort to live in peace with all men and to be holy, for I know that without holiness no one will see You, Lord. I purpose to see to it that I do not miss Your grace and that no bitter root grows up within me to cause trouble and defile me.

I will watch and pray that I enter not into temptation or cause others to stumble.

Thank You, Father, that You watch over Your Word to perform it and that whom the Son has set free is free indeed. I declare that I have overcome resentment and bitterness by the blood of the Lamb, and by the word of my testimony.

In Jesus' name, amen.

Scripture References

Ephesians 4:31 AMP	Ephesians 4:31,32 NIV
Luke 4:18	Hebrews 12:14,15 NIV
Isaiah 10:27	Matthew 26:41
Proverbs 11:14	Romans 14:21
John 15:26 AMP	Jeremiah 1:12 AMP
Philippians 2:12,13 NIV	John 8:36
Matthew 5:44	Revelation 12:11

78

∽ Twenty-Two ∼

Health and Healing

Father, in the name of Jesus, I confess Your Word concerning healing. As I do this, I believe and say that Your Word will not return to You void, but will accomplish what it says it will. Therefore, I believe in the name of Jesus that I am healed, according to 1 Peter 2:24. It is written in Your Word that Jesus Himself took our infirmities and bore our sicknesses. Therefore, with great boldness and confidence I say on the authority of that written Word that I am redeemed from the curse of sickness, and I refuse to tolerate its symptoms.

Satan, I speak to you in the name of Jesus and say that your principalities, powers, your spirits who rule the present darkness, and your spiritual wickedness in heavenly places are bound from operating against me in any way. I am the property of Almighty God, and I give you no place in me. I dwell in the secret place of the Most High God. I abide, remain stable and fixed under the shadow of the Almighty, whose power no foe can withstand.

Now, Father, because I reverence and worship You, I have the assurance of Your Word that the angel of the Lord encamps around about me and delivers me from every evil work. No evil shall befall me, no plague or calamity shall come near my dwelling. I confess the Word of God abides in me and delivers to me perfect soundness of mind and wholeness in body and spirit from the deepest parts of my nature in my immortal spirit even to the joints and marrow of my bones. That Word is medication and life to my flesh for the law of the Spirit of life operates in me and makes me free from the law of sin and death.

I have on the whole armor of God, and the shield of faith protects me from all the fiery darts of the wicked. Jesus is the High Priest of my confession, and I hold fast to my confession of faith in Your Word. I stand immovable and fixed in full assurance that I have health and healing now in the name of Jesus. Amen.

Once this has been prayed, thank the Father that Satan is bound and continue to confess this healing and thank God for it.

Scripture References

Isaiah 55:11	Psalm 91:10
1 Peter 2:24	Psalm 34:7
Matthew 8:17	2 Timothy 1:7
Galatians 3:13	Hebrews 4:12,14
James 4:7	Proverbs 4:22
Ephesians 6:12	Romans 8:2
2 Corinthians 10:4	Ephesians 6:11,16
Psalm 91:1	Psalm 112:7

ᕱ Twenty-Three ᕱ

Safety

Father, in the name of Jesus, I thank You that You watch over Your Word to perform it. I thank You that I dwell in the secret place of the Most High and that I remain stable and fixed under the shadow of the Almighty whose power no foe can withstand.

Father, You are my refuge and my fortress. *No evil shall befall me — no accident shall overtake me — nor any plague or calamity come near my home.* You give Your angels special charge over me, to accompany and defend and preserve me in all my ways of obedience and service. They are encamped around about me.

Father, You are my confidence, firm and strong. You keep my foot from being caught in a trap or hidden danger. Father, You give me safety and ease me — *Jesus is my safety!*

Traveling — As I go, I say, "Let me pass over to the other side," and I have what I say. I walk on my way securely and in confident trust, for my heart and mind are firmly fixed and stayed on You, and I am kept in perfect peace.

81

Sleeping — Father, I sing for joy upon my bed because You sustain me. In peace I lie down and sleep, for You alone, Lord, make me dwell in safety. I lie down and I am not afraid. My sleep is sweet for You give blessings to me in sleep. Thank You, Father, in Jesus' name. Amen.

Continue to feast and meditate upon all of Psalm 91 for yourself and your loved ones!

Scripture References

Jeremiah 1:12

Psalm 91:1,2 AMP

Psalm 91:10 AMP

Psalm 91:11 AMP

Psalm 34:7

Proverbs 3:26 AMP

Isaiah 49:25

Mark 4:35

Proverbs 3:23 AMP

Psalm 112:7

Isaiah 26:3

Psalm 149:5

Psalm 3:5

Psalm 4:8 AMP

Proverbs 3:24

Psalm 127:2

82

✧ Twenty-Four ✧

Peaceful Sleep

In the name of Jesus, I bind you, Satan, and all your agents from my dreams. I forbid you to interfere in any way with my sleep.

I bring every thought, every imagination, and every dream into the captivity and obedience of Jesus Christ. Father, I thank You that even as I sleep my heart counsels me and reveals to me Your purpose and plan. Thank You for sweet sleep, for You promised Your beloved sweet sleep. Therefore, my heart is glad, and my spirit rejoices. My body and soul rest and confidently dwell in safety. Amen.

83

Scripture References

Matthew 16:19	*Psalm 16:7-9*
Matthew 18:18	*Psalm 127:2*
2 Corinthians 10:5	*Proverbs 3:24*

∽ *Twenty-Five* ∾

Prosperity

Father, in the name of Your Son, Jesus, I confess Your Word over my finances this day. As I do this, I say it with my mouth and believe it in my heart and know that Your Word will not return to You void, but will accomplish what it says it will do.

Therefore, I believe in the name of Jesus that all my needs are met, according to Philippians 4:19. I believe that because I have given tithes and offerings to further Your cause, Father, gifts will be given to me, good measure, pressed down, shaken together, and running over will they pour into my bosom. For with the measure I deal out, it will be measured back to me.

Father, You have delivered me out of the authority of darkness into the Kingdom of Your dear Son. Father, I have taken my place as Your child. I thank You that You have assumed Your place as my Father and have made Your home with me. You are taking care of me and even now are enabling me to walk in love and in wisdom, and to walk in the fullness of fellowship with Your Son.

84

Satan, I bind you from my finances, according to Matthew 18:18, and loose you from your assignment against me, in the name of Jesus.

Father, I thank You that Your ministering spirits are now free to minister for me and bring in the necessary finances.

Father, I confess You are a very present help in trouble, and You are more than enough. I confess, God, You are able to make all grace — every favor and earthly blessing — come to me in abundance, so that I am always, and in all circumstances furnished in abundance for every good work and charitable donation. Amen.

Scripture References

Isaiah 55:11	2 Corinthians 6:16,18
Philippians 4:19	Matthew 18:18
Luke 6:38	Hebrews 1:14
Mark 10:29,30	2 Corinthians 9:8 AMP
Colossians 1:13	Psalm 46:1

85

Twenty-Six

To Receive the Infilling of the Holy Spirit

My heavenly Father, I am Your child, for I believe in my heart that Jesus has been raised from the dead and I have confessed Him as my Lord.

Jesus said, "How much more shall your heavenly Father give the Holy Spirit to those who ask Him." I ask You now in the name of Jesus to fill me with the Holy Spirit. I step into the fullness and power that I desire in the name of Jesus. I confess that I am a Spirit-filled Christian. As I yield my vocal organs, I expect to speak in tongues for the Spirit gives me utterance in the name of Jesus. Praise the Lord! Amen.

86

Scripture References

John 14:16,17

Luke 11:13

Acts 1:8a

Acts 2:4

Acts 2:32,33,39

Acts 8:12-17

Acts 10:44-46

Acts 19:2,5,6

1 Corinthians 14:2-15

1 Corinthians 14:18,27

Ephesians 6:18

Jude 1:20

✨ Twenty-Seven ✨

When Desiring to Have a Baby

Our Father, my spouse and I bow our knees unto You. Father of our Lord Jesus Christ of whom the whole family in heaven and on earth is named, we pray that You would grant to us according to the riches of Your glory, to be strengthened with might by Your Spirit in the inner man. Christ dwells in our hearts by faith, that we — being rooted and grounded in love — may be able to comprehend with all the saints what is the breadth, and length, and depth, and height of the love of Christ, which passes knowledge, that we might be filled with all the fullness of God.

Hallelujah, we praise You, O Lord, for You give children to the childless wife, so that she becomes a happy mother. And we thank You that You are the One Who is building our family. As Your children and inheritors through Jesus Christ, we receive Your gift — the fruit of the womb, Your child as our reward.

We praise You, our Father, in Jesus' name, for we know that whatsoever we ask, we receive of

87

You, because we keep Your commandments, and do those things which are pleasing in Your sight.

Thank You, Father, that we are a fruitful vine within our house; our children will be like olive shoots around our table. Thus shall we be blessed because we fear the Lord.

In Jesus' name we pray, amen.

Scripture References

Ephesians 3:14-19

Psalm 113:9 AMP

Psalm 127:3

1 John 3:22,23 AMP

Psalm 128:3,4 AMP

Twenty-Eight

Godly Order in Pregnancy and Childbirth

Father, in Jesus' name, I confess Your Word this day over my pregnancy and the birth of my child. I ask that You will quickly perform Your Word trusting that it will not go out from You and return to You void, but rather that it will accomplish that which pleases You. Your Word is quick and powerful, and discerns my heart intentions and the thoughts of my mind.

Right now I put on the whole armor of God so that I may be able to stand against the tricks and traps of the devil. I recognize that my fight is not with flesh and blood, but against principalities, powers and the rulers of darkness and spiritual wickedness in high places. God, I stand above all, taking the shield of faith and being able to quench the attacks of the devil with Your mighty power. I stand in faith during this pregnancy and birth, not giving any room to fear, but possessing power, love and a sound mind as Your Word promises in 2 Timothy 1:7.

Heavenly Father, I confess that You are my refuge; I trust You during this pregnancy and childbirth. I am thankful that You have put angels at watch over me and my unborn child. I cast all the care and burden of this pregnancy over on You, Lord. Your grace is sufficient for me through this pregnancy; You strengthen my weaknesses.

Father, Your Word declares that my unborn child was created in Your image, fearfully and wonderfully made to praise You. You have made me a joyful mother, and I am blessed with a heritage from You as my reward. I commit this child to You, Father, and pray that he will grow and call me blessed.

I am not afraid of pregnancy or childbirth because I am fixed and trusting upon You, Father. I believe that my pregnancy and childbirth will be void of all problems. Thank You, Father, that all decisions regarding my pregnancy and delivery will be godly, that the Holy Spirit will intervene. Lord, You are my dwelling place and I rest in the knowledge that evil will not come near me and no sickness or infirmity will strike me or my unborn child. I know that Jesus died on the cross to take away my sickness and pain. Having accepted Your Son Jesus as my Savior, I confess that my child will be born healthy and completely whole. Thank You, Father, for the law of the

Spirit of life in Christ Jesus that has made me and my child free from the law of sin and death!

Father, thank You for protecting me and my baby and for our good health. Thank You for hearing and answering my prayers. Amen.

Scripture References

Jeremiah 1:12

Isaiah 55:11

Hebrews 4:12

Ephesians 6:11,12,16

Psalm 91:2,11

1 Peter 5:7

2 Corinthians 12:9

Genesis 1:26

Psalm 139:14

Psalm 113:9

Psalm 127:3

Proberbs 31:28

Psalm 112:7

Psalm 91:1,10

Matthew 8:17

Romans 8:2

James 4:7

Ephesians 6:12

John 4:13

Matthew 18:18

Jeremiah 33:3

∽ Twenty-Nine ∽

Adopting a Child

Father, in Jesus' name, we come boldly before Your throne of grace that we may receive mercy and find grace to help in our time of need. We are trusting in You, and seek to do good; so that we may dwell in the land, and feed surely on Your faithfulness.

We delight ourselves also in You, and You give us the desires and secret petitions of our heart. We believe our desire to adopt a child is from You, and we are willing to assume the responsibility of rearing this child in the ways of the Master.

Father, we commit our way to You [roll and repose each care of our load on You]. Our confidence is in You, and You will bring this adoption to pass according to Your purpose and plan.

Lord, Your Son Jesus demonstrated Your love for children when He said, **"Let the children alone, don't prevent them from coming to me. God's kingdom is made up of people like these"** (Matt. 19:14 MESSAGE). Then, He laid hands on them and blessed them.

92

Use us as Your instruments of peace and righteousness to bless this child. We purpose in our hearts to train this child up in the way that he/she should go.

Lord, we are embracing this child (Your best gift) as our very own with Your love, as Jesus said, **"Whoever embraces one of these children as I do embraces me, and far more than me — God who sent me"** (Mark 9:37 MESSAGE).

Father, take this child up and be a Father and Mother to him/her as we extend our hands and our hearts to embrace him/her. Thank You for the blood of Jesus that gives protection to this one whom we love.

We thank You for the man and woman who conceived this child, and pray that You will bless them, cause Your face to shine upon them, and be merciful to them. If they do not know Jesus, we ask You, the Lord of the harvest, to send forth laborers to share truth with them that they may come out of the snare of the devil.

Mercy and truth are written upon the tablets of our hearts, and You cause us to find favor and good understanding with You and with man — the adoption agency staff, the judges, and all those who are involved in this decision-making process. May everyone be careful that they do not despise one of these little ones over whom they have

93

jurisdiction — for they have angels who see Your face continually in heaven.

We believe that all our words are righteous (upright and in right standing with You, Father). By our long forbearing and calmness of spirit those in authority are persuaded, and our soft speech breaks down the most bonelike resistance.

Lord, we are looking to You as our Great Counselor and Mighty Advocate. We ask for Your wisdom for us and our attorneys.

Father, contend with those who contend with us, and give safety to our child and ease him/her day by day. We are calling on You, in the name of Jesus, and You will answer us and show us great and mighty things. No weapon formed against us and this adoption shall prosper, and any tongue that rises against us in judgment we shall show to be in the wrong. This [peace, righteousness, security, and triumph over opposition] is our inheritance as Your children.

Father, we believe, therefore we have spoken. May it be done unto us according to Your Word.

In Jesus' name, amen.

94

Scripture References

Hebrews 4:16

Psalm 37:3

Psalm 37:4 AMP

Ephesians 6:4 MESSAGE

Psalm 37:5 AMP

Proverbs 22:6

Psalm 67:1

Matthew 9:38

2 Timothy 2:26

Proverbs 3:3,4

Matthew 18:10 PHILLIPS

Proverbs 8:8 AMP

Proverbs 25:15 AMP

James 1:5

Isaiah 49:25

Jeremiah 33:3

Isaiah 54:17 AMP

Psalm 116:10

Luke 1:38

95

Part II

Prayers for Relationships

Thirty

Developing Healthy Friendships

Father, help me to meet new friends — friends who will encourage me. May I find in these friendships the companionship and fellowship You have ordained for me. I know that You are my source of love, companionship, and friendship. Your love and friendship are expressed through my relationship with You and members of the Body of Christ.

According to Proverbs 27:17 CEV, iron sharpens iron, so friends sharpen the minds of each other. As we learn from each other, may we find a worthy purpose in our relationship. Keep me well balanced in my friendships, so that I will always please You rather than pleasing other people.

I ask for divine connections — good friendships ordained by You. Thank You for the courage and grace to let go of detrimental friendships. I ask and receive, by faith, discernment for developing healthy relationships. Your Word says that two are better

99

than one, because if one falls, there will be someone to lift that person up.

Father, You know the hearts of people, so I won't be deceived by outward appearances. Bad friendships corrupt good morals. Thank You for quality friends who help me build a stronger character and draw me closer to You. Help me be a friend to others and to love my friends at all times. I will laugh with those who laugh, I will rejoice with those who rejoice, and I will weep with those who weep. Teach me what I need to know to be a quality friend.

Develop in me a fun personality and a good sense of humor. Help me to relax around people and to be myself — the person You created me to be. Instruct my heart and mold my character, that I may be faithful and trustworthy over the friendships You are sending into my life.

100

Father, Your Son Jesus is my best Friend. He is a Friend Who sticks closer than a brother. He defined the standard when He said in John 15:13, **Greater love hath no man than this, that a man lay down his life for his friends.**

Thank You, Lord, that I can entrust myself and my need for friends into Your keeping. I submit to the leadership of the Holy Spirit, in the name of Jesus. Amen.

This prayer is composed of Scriptures and writings taken from "Meeting New Friends," *Prayers That Avail Much for Teens!* (Tulsa: Harrison House, 1991), pp. 50-52.

Scripture References

Proverbs 13:20 *NIV*

Ephesians 5:30 *NIV*

Philippians 2:2,3 *NIV*

Proverbs 13:20 *NIV*

Psalm 84:11 *NIV*

Ecclesiastes 4:9,10 *NIV*

1 Corinthians 15:33 *AMP*

James 1:17 *NIV*

Proverbs 17:17

Romans 12:15

Proverbs 18:24

Psalm 37:4,5 *NIV*

Thirty-One

Maintaining Good Relations

Father, in the name of Jesus, I will not withhold good from those to whom it is due [its rightful owners], when it is in the power of my hand to do it. I will render to all men their dues. I will [pay] taxes to whom taxes are due, revenue to whom revenue is due, respect to whom respect is due, and honor to whom honor is due.

I will not lose heart and grow weary and faint in acting nobly and doing nobly and right, for in due season I shall reap, if I do not loosen and relax my courage and faint. So then, as occasion and opportunity open up to me, I will do good [morally] to all people [not only being useful or profitable to them, but also doing what is for their spiritual good and advantage]. I am mindful to be a blessing, especially to those of the household of faith [those who belong to God's family with me, the believers].

I will not contend with a man for no reason — when he has done me no wrong. If possible, as far as it depends on me, I purpose to live at peace with everyone. Amen.

Scripture References

Proverbs 3:27 AMP

Romans 13:7 AMP

Galatians 6:9,10 AMP

Proverbs 3:30 AMP

Romans 12:18 AMP

Thirty-Two

Improving Communication Skills

Introduction

Lack of communication skills is one of the greatest hindrances to healthy relationships. Most of the time, when we pray, we are seeking change. We cannot change others, but we can submit to the constant ministry of transformation by the Holy Spirit. (Rom. 12:1,2.)

Prayer prepares us for change. Change produces change, which may be uncomfortable. If we will move through the discomfort, God will work with us, leading us out of our self-developed defense mechanisms into a place of victory. In this place He heals our brokenness, becomes our defense and our vindication. We are enabled to submit to the Champion of our salvation, which we are working out with fear and trembling. (Phil. 2:12.)

Adults who grew up in judgmental, critical homes where they were never allowed to express themselves sometimes carry much hurt and anger into their relationships. Often, they were not permitted to have their own feelings without being condemned; they were not permitted to explore any ideas different from their parents or caregivers. There was an eye watching their every move. Any punishment they received was justified. Their parents were incapable of making a mistake.

Adult children of religiously rigid environments were led to believe that any slip, error in judgment, or mistake was a sin that would send them straight to hell; the parent's religious doctrine was the only way to heaven; and to deviate from it would lead to destruction. Forgiveness could be attained only after much sorrow, penance, and retribution. Death before the completion of repentance led to an eternity in hell.

People raised in such oppressive home environments were never allowed to find themselves or to travel their own individual spiritual journeys leading to truth. Their parents, especially the father-figure in the home, was God in the flesh. Conflict resolution was never taught or practiced. Whatever the head of the household said was law — and disobedience to his law was not discussed, but beaten out of the child. The wife was subservient and was not allowed to question the dictates of the husband.

When these adults marry, they often feel that they have finally found a platform from

105

which to express themselves. They have escaped a place of abiding fear, constant condemnation, and continual criticism. Having no communication skills, they often have difficulty expressing themselves properly. When anyone disagrees with them, they tend to react as they were taught. Only now, the marriage partner or friend does not submit to dogmatic, manipulative words. Frustration develops. The adult child seeks to make himself or herself understood, resulting in more frustration. Anger is fed, and the individual continues to be in bondage to the idea that he or she should never have been born. The person either retreats to a silent corner, refusing to talk, or uses words to build walls of defense — shutting others out. He or she resides inside emotional isolation, attempting to remove himself or herself from more hurt and criticism.

106

There is a way of escape. God sent His Word to heal us and to deliver us from all our destructions. (Ps. 107:20.) We must determine to listen, to learn, and to change with the help of the Holy Spirit — our Teacher, our Guide, and our Intercessor. The anointing is upon Jesus to bind up and heal our emotional wounds. (Luke 4:18.) His anointing destroys every yoke of bondage (Isa. 10:27), setting the captives free.

Prayer

Father, I am Your child. Jesus said that if I pray to You in secret, You will reward me openly.

Father, I desire with all my heart to walk in love, but I am ever sabotaging my own efforts and failing in my relationships. I know that without faith it is impossible to please and be satisfactory to You. I am coming near to You, believing that You exist and that You are the rewarder of those who earnestly and diligently seek You.

Show "me" to me. Uncover — bring everything to the light — when anything is exposed and reproved by the light, it is made visible and clear; and where everything is visible and clear there is light.

Heal the past wounds and hurts which have controlled my behavior and my speech. Teach me to guard my heart with all diligence, for out of it flow the very issues of life. Teach me to speak the truth in love in my home, in my church, with my friends and in all my relationships. Also, help me to realize that others have a right to express themselves. Help me to make room for their ideas, their opinions, even when they are different from mine.

Words are powerful. The power of life and death is in the tongue, and You said that I would eat the fruit of it.

107

Father, I realize that words can be creative or destructive. A word out of my mouth may seem of no account, but it can accomplish nearly anything — or destroy it! A careless or wrongly placed word out of my mouth can set off a forest fire. By my speech I can ruin the world, turn harmony to chaos, throw mud on a reputation, send the whole world up in smoke, and go up in smoke with it, smoke right from the pit of hell. This is scary!

Father, forgive me for speaking curses and blessings. I am reacting out of past hurts and unresolved anger. At times I am dogmatic, even boasting that I am wise; sometimes, unknowingly I have twisted the truth to make myself sound wise; at times I have tried to look better than others, or get the better of another; my words have contributed to things falling apart. My human anger is misdirected and works unrighteousness.

Father, forgive me. I cannot change myself, but I am willing to change and walk in the wisdom that is from above.

Father, I submit to that wisdom from above that begins with a holy life and is characterized by getting along with others. It is gentle and reasonable, overflowing with mercy and blessings, not hot one day and cold the next, not two-faced. Use me as Your instrument to develop a healthy, robust

108

community that lives right with You. I will enjoy its results only if I do the hard work of getting along with others, treating them with dignity and honor.

With the help of the Holy Spirit and by Your grace, I will not let any unwholesome talk come out of my mouth, but only what is helpful for building others up according to their needs, that it may benefit those who listen.

My heart overflows with a goodly theme; I address my psalm to You, the King. My tongue is like the pen of a ready writer. Mercy and kindness shut out all hatred and selfishness, and truth shuts out all deliberate hypocrisy or falsehood; and I bind them about my neck, write them upon the tablet of my heart.

I speak excellent and princely things; and the opening of my lips shall be for right things. My mouth shall utter truth, and wrongdoing is detestable and loathsome to my lips. All the words of my mouth are righteous (upright and in right standing with You, Lord); there is nothing contrary to truth or crooked in them. My tongue is as choice silver, and my lips feed and guide many. I open my mouth in skillful and godly wisdom, and on my tongue is the law of kindness [giving counsel and instruction].

Father, thank You for loving me unconditionally. I thank You for sending Your Son Jesus to be my Friend and elder Brother and for giving me

109

Your Holy Spirit to teach me and to bring all things to my remembrance. I am an overcomer by the blood of the Lamb, and by the word of my testimony.

In the name of Jesus I pray, amen.

Scripture References

1 John 3:1	Ephesians 4:29 *NIV*
Matthew 6:6	Psalm 45:1 *AMP*
Hebrews 11:6 *AMP*	Proverbs 3:3 *AMP*
Ephesians 5:13 *AMP*	Proverbs 8:6-8 *AMP*
Proverbs 4:23	Proverbs 10:20,21 *AMP*
Ephesians 4:15	Proverbs 31:26 *AMP*
Proverbs 18:21	Romans 8:31-39 *NIV*
James 3:5,6 *MESSAGE*	Hebrews 2:11 *NIV*
James 3:9-16 *MESSAGE*	John 15:15 *NIV*
James 3:17	John 14:26
James 3:17,18 *MESSAGE*	Revelation 12:11

~ *Thirty-Three* ~

Finding Favor With Others

Father, in the name of Jesus, You make Your face to shine upon and enlighten _____ and are gracious (kind, merciful, and giving favor) to him/her. _____ is the head and not the tail. _____ is above only and not beneath.

Thank You for favor for _____ who seeks Your Kingdom and Your righteousness and diligently seeks good. _____ is a blessing to You, Lord, and is a blessing to _____ *(name them: family, neighbors, business associates, etc.)*. Grace (favor) is with _____ who loves the Lord Jesus in sincerity. _____ extends favor, honor, and love to _____ *(names)*. _____ is flowing in Your Love, Father. You are pouring out upon _____ the spirit of favor. You crown him/her with glory and honor for he/she is Your child — Your workmanship.

_____ is a success today. _____ is someone very special with You, Lord. _____ is growing in the Lord — waxing strong in spirit. Father, You give _____ knowledge and skill in all learning and wisdom.

You bring _____ to find favor, compassion, and lovingkindness with _____ *(names)*. _____ obtains favor in the sight of all who look upon him/her this day in the name of Jesus. _____ is filled with Your fullness — rooted and grounded in love. You are doing exceeding abundantly above all that _____ asks or thinks for Your mighty power is taking over in _____.

Thank You, Father, that _____ is well-favored by You and by man in Jesus' name! Amen.

Scripture References

Numbers 6:25	Psalm 8:5
Deuteronomy 28:13	Ephesians 2:10
Matthew 6:33	Luke 2:40
Proverbs 11:27	Daniel 1:17
Ephesians 6:24	Daniel 1:9
Luke 6:38	Esther 2:15,17
Zachariah 12:10	Ephesians 3:19,20

∽ Thirty-Four ∾

Finding a Mate

Introduction

In our ministry we hear from many men and women who desire to be married. If that is your desire, we encourage you to ask the Lord to prepare you for marriage. Submit to God's future plans for your life, and purpose to please Him. Do not make your deliberations, without knowing His will, at the expense of your personal spiritual growth and transformation. Going from glory to glory (2 Cor. 3:18) is not dependent on having a spouse.

Most of the time, each partner brings a lot of emotional baggage into the marriage relationship. As you prepare for marriage, remember that the anointing that was upon Jesus (Luke 4:18,19) is within you. This anointing will destroy every yoke of bondage (Isa. 10:27) as God exposes emotional wounds and heals your brokenness.

Knowing the reality of your completeness in Christ Jesus will enable you to enter into a healthy relationship, one in which both you and your

113

partner will grow together spiritually and in every other area of life. Seeking first the Kingdom of God and His righteousness (Matt. 6:33), doing those things that are pleasing in His sight (1 John 3:22), will prepare you to be the person designed by Him to fulfill the role of husband or wife.

This prayer is written for your own growth and benefit.

Prayer

Father, I come before You in the name of Jesus, asking for Your will to be done in my life as I look to You for a marriage partner. I submit to the constant ministry of transformation by the Holy Spirit, making my petition known to You.

114

Prepare me for marriage by bringing everything to light that has been hidden — wounded emotions, walls of denial, emotional isolation, silence or excessive talking, anger or rigidity [*name any wall that separates you from healthy relationships and God's love and grace*]. The weapons of my warfare are not carnal, but mighty through You, Lord, to the pulling down of strongholds.

I know the One in Whom I have placed my confidence, and I am perfectly certain that the work, whether I remain unmarried or marry, is safe in Your hands until that day.

Because I love You, Lord, and because I am called according to Your plan, everything that happens to me fits into a pattern for good. In Your foreknowledge, You chose me to bear the family likeness of Your Son. You chose me long ago; when the time came You called me, You made me righteous in Your sight, and then lifted me to the splendor of life as Your child.

Since I am surrounded by such a great cloud of witnesses, let me throw off everything that hinders and the sin that so easily entangles, and let me run with perseverance the race marked out for me. Let me fix my eyes on Jesus, the Author and Perfecter of my faith, Who for the joy set before Him endured the cross, scorning its shame, and sat down at the right hand of Your throne, O God. I consider Him Who endured such opposition from sinful men, so that I will not grow weary and lose heart.

I turn my back on the turbulent desires of youth and give my positive attention to goodness, integrity, love, and peace in company with all those who approach You, Lord, in sincerity. I have nothing to do with silly and ill-informed controversies which lead inevitably to strife. As Your servant, I am not a person of strife. I seek to be kind to all, ready and able to teach. I seek to be tolerant and have the ability gently to correct those who oppose Your message.

Father, I desire and earnestly seek (aim at and strive after) first of all Your Kingdom and Your righteousness (Your way of doing and being right), and then all these things taken together will be given me besides. So I do not worry and will not be anxious about tomorrow.

I am persuaded that I can trust You because You first loved me. You chose me in Christ before the foundation of the world. In Him the whole fullness of Deity (the Godhead) continues to dwell in bodily form [giving complete expression of the divine nature] and I am in Him, made full and have come to the fullness of life [in Christ].

I am filled with the Godhead — Father, Son, and Holy Spirit — and I reach toward full spiritual stature. And He (Christ) is the Head of all rule and authority [of every angelic principality and power]. So, because of Jesus, I am complete; Jesus is my Lord.

I come before You, Father, expressing my desire for a Christian mate. I petition that Your will be done in my life. Now I enter into that blessed rest by adhering to, trusting in, and relying on You.

In Jesus' name, amen.

Scripture References

Matthew 6:10

1 Corinthians 4:5

2 Corinthians 10:4

2 Timothy 1:12 PHILLIPS

Romans 8:28-30 PHILLIPS

Hebrews 12:1-3 NIV

2 Timothy 2:22-25
  PHILLIPS

Matthew 6:33,34 AMP

1 John 4:19

Ephesians 1:4

Colossians 2:9,10 AMP

Matthew 6:10

Hebrews 4:10

John 14:1 AMP

~ Thirty-Five ~

Preparing Self for Marriage

Father, sometimes being single can be so lonely, so painful. Seeing people in pairs, laughing and having fun, makes me feel even more alone and different.

Lord, please comfort me in these times. Help me to deal with my feelings and thoughts in an appropriate way. Help me to remember to work hard on myself, so that I will be whole and mature when You bring the right person into my life.

Help me to remember that this is a time of preparation for the day when I will be joined to another human being for life. Show me how to be responsible for myself and how to allow others to be responsible for themselves.

Teach me about boundaries, what they are and how to establish them instead of walls. Teach me about love, Your love, and how to speak the truth in love, as Jesus did.

Father, I don't want to be a hindrance to my future spouse, to You, or to myself. Help me to take a good look at myself, at my self-image. Lead me to people — teachers, preachers, counselors — and to things — books, tapes, seminars — anyone and anything You can use to teach me Your ways of being and doing right and being whole.

Teach me how to choose the mate You would have for me. Give me the wisdom I need to see clearly, and not to be double-minded. Help me to recognize the qualities You would have me look for in a mate.

Father, thank You for revealing to me that the choice of a mate is not to be based only on emotions and feelings, but that You have very definite guidelines in the Bible for me to use. I know that when I put these principles into practice, I will save myself a lot of pain and trouble.

Thank You that You are not trying to make things hard for me, but that You know me better than I know myself. You know my situation — You know the beginning from the end. You know the qualities and attributes that are needed in another person that will make me happy in our shared life together and that person happy with me.

119

I pray that you will keep my foot from being caught in a hidden trap of danger. I cast the care of this decision on You, knowing that You will cause my thoughts to come in line with Your will so that my plans will be established and succeed.

In Jesus' name I pray, amen.

Scripture References

1 Corinthians 1:3,4 NIV	James 1:5-8
Ephesians 4:15	Proverbs 3:26 AMP
Matthew 6:33 AMP	Proverbs 16:3 AMP

⌒ Thirty-Six ⌒

Compatibility in Marriage

Father, in the name of Jesus, I pray and confess that my spouse and I endure long and are patient and kind; that we are never envious and never boil over with jealousy. We are not boastful or vainglorious, and we do not display ourselves haughtily. We are not conceited or arrogant and inflated with pride. We are not rude and unmannerly, and we do not act unbecomingly. We do not insist on our own rights or our own way, for we are not self-seeking or touchy or fretful or resentful. We take no account of the evil done to us and pay no attention to a suffered wrong. We do not rejoice at injustice and unrighteousness, but we rejoice when right and truth prevail.

We bear up under anything and everything that comes. We are ever ready to believe the best of each other. Our hopes are fadeless under all circumstances. We endure everything without weakening. *Our love never fails* — it never fades out or becomes obsolete or comes to an end.

We are confessing that our lives and our family's lives lovingly express truth in all things that we speak truly, deal truly, and live truly. We are enfolded in love and have grown up in every way and in all things. We esteem and delight in one another, forgiving one another readily and freely as God in Christ has forgiven us. We are imitators of God and copy His example as well-beloved children imitate their father.

Thank You, Father, that our marriage grows stronger each day because it is founded on Your Word and on Your kind of love. We give You the praise for it all, Father, in the name of Jesus. Amen.

Scripture References

1 Corinthians 13:4-8 AMP	Ephesians 4:15,32
1 Corinthians 14:1	Ephesians 5:1,2

∽ *Thirty-Seven* ∾

Wives

Father, in the name of Jesus, I take Your Word and speak it out of my mouth and say that I have faith that I am a capable, intelligent, patient, and virtuous woman. I am far more precious than jewels. My value to my husband and family is far above rubies and pearls.

The heart of my husband trusts in me confidently and relies on and believes in me completely, so that he has no lack of honest gain or need of dishonest spoil.

Father, I will comfort, encourage, and do him only good as long as there is life within me. I gird myself with strength and spiritual, mental, and physical fitness for my God-given task. I taste and see that my gain from work with and for God is good. My lamp goes not out; it burns on continually through the night of any trouble, privation, or sorrow, and it warns away fear, doubt, and distrust.

I open my hand to the poor. I reach out my filled hands to the needy — whether in spirit, soul, or body. My husband is known as a success in everything he puts his hand to. Strength and dignity are my clothing, and my position in my household is strong. I am secure and at peace in knowing that my family is in readiness for the future.

I open my mouth with skillful and godly wisdom, and in my tongue is the law of kindness and love. I look well to how things go in my household. The bread of idleness, gossip, discontent, and self-pity I will not eat.

My children rise up and call me blessed and happy. My husband boasts of and praises me, saying that I excel in all that I set my hand to. I am a woman who reverently and worshipfully loves You, Lord, and You shall give me the fruits of my hands. My works will praise me wherever I go, for Father, I confess that I am a submitted wife — simply because I want to be and I recognize Your authority. I thank You for my husband who is head over me, but who has given me (through the chain of command) the necessary power to do what Your Word says for me to do from Proverbs 31:10-31. I am as this woman is — a loving, successful, submitted wife — in the name of Jesus. Amen.

Scripture Reference
Proverbs 31:10-31 AMP

124

Thirty-Eight

The Unborn Child

Father, in Jesus' name, I thank You for my unborn child. I treasure this child as a gift from You. My child was created in Your image, perfectly healthy and complete. You have known my child since conception and know the path he/she will take with his/her life. I ask Your blessing upon him/her and stand and believe in his/her salvation through Jesus Christ.

When You created man and woman, You called them blessed and crowned them with glory and honor. It is in You, Father, that my child will live and move, and have his/her being. He/she is Your offspring and will come to worship and praise You.

125

Heavenly Father, I thank and praise You for the great things You have done and are continuing to do. I am in awe at the miracle of life You have placed inside of me. Thank You! Amen.

Scripture References

Psalm 127:3

Genesis 1:26

Jeremiah 1:5

2 Peter 3:9

Psalm 8:5

Acts 17:28,29

Matthew 18:18

John 14:13

Galatians 3:13

1 John 3:8

Psalm 91:1

∽ Thirty-Nine ∾

The Children

Father, in the name of Jesus, I pray and confess Your Word over my children and surround them with my faith — faith in Your Word that You watch over it to perform it! I confess and believe that my children are disciples of Christ taught of the Lord and obedient to Your will. Great is the peace and undisturbed composure of my children, because You, God, contend with that which contends with my children, and You give them safety and ease them.

Father, You will perfect that which concerns me. *I commit and cast the care of my children once and for all over on You, Father.* They are in Your hands, and I am positively persuaded that You are able to guard and keep that which I have committed to You. You are more than enough!

I confess that my children obey their parents in the Lord as His representatives, because this is just and right. My children _____ honor, esteem, and value as precious their parents; for this is the first commandment with a promise: that all may be well with my children and that they may live long on earth. I believe and confess that my children choose life and love You, Lord, obey Your voice, and cling to You; for You are their life and the length of their days. Therefore, my children are the head and not the tail, and shall be above only and not beneath. They are blessed when they come in and when they go out.

I believe and confess that You give Your angels charge over my children to accompany and defend and preserve them in all their ways. You, Lord, are their refuge and fortress. You are their glory and the lifter of their heads.

As parents, we will not provoke, irritate, or fret our children. We will not be hard on them or harass them, or cause them to become discouraged, sullen, or morose, or feel inferior and frustrated. We will not break or wound their spirits, but we will rear them tenderly in the training, discipline, counsel, and admonition of the Lord. We will train them in the way they should go, and when they are old they will not depart from it.

O Lord, my Lord, how excellent (majestic and glorious) is Your name in all the earth! You have set Your glory on or above the heavens. Out of the mouth of babes and unweaned infants You have established strength because of Your foes, that You might silence the enemy and the avenger. I sing praise to Your name, O Most High. *The enemy is turned back from my children in the name of Jesus!* They increase in wisdom and in favor with God and man. Amen.

Scripture References

Jeremiah 1:12	*Psalm 91:11*
Isaiah 54:13	*Psalm 91:2*
Isaiah 49:25	*Psalm 3:3*
1 Peter 5:7	*Colossians 3:21*
2 Timothy 1:12	*Ephesians 6:4*
Ephesians 6:1-3	*Proverbs 22:6*
Deuteronomy 30:19,20	*Psalm 8:1,2*
Deuteronomy 28:13	*Psalm 9:2,3*
Deuteronomy 28:3,6	*Luke 2:52*

129

∽ Forty ∾

Child's Future

Father, Your Word declares that children are an inheritance from You and promises peace when they are taught in Your ways. I dedicate _____ to You today, that he/she might be raised as You would desire and will follow the path You would choose. Father, I confess Your Word this day over _____. I thank You that Your Word goes out and will not return unto You void, but will accomplish what it says it will do.

Heavenly Father, I commit myself, as a parent, to train _____ in the way he/she should go, trusting in the promise that he/she will not depart from Your ways, but will grow and prosper in them. I turn the care and burden of raising him/her over to You. I will not provoke my child, but will nurture and love him/her in Your care. I will do as the Word of God commands and teach my child diligently. My child will be upon my heart and mind. Your grace is sufficient to overcome my inabilities as a parent.

My child _____ is obedient and honors both his/her parents, being able to accept the abundant promises of Your Word of long life and prosperity. _____ is a godly child; not ashamed or afraid to honor and keep Your Word. He/She stands convinced that You are the Almighty God. I am thankful that as _____ grows, he/she will remember You and not pass by the opportunity of a relationship with Your Son, Jesus. Your great blessings will be upon _____ for keeping Your ways. I thank You for Your blessings over every area of _____'s life, that You will see to the salvation and obedience of his/her life to Your ways.

Heavenly Father, I thank You now that laborers will be sent into _____'s path, preparing the way for salvation, as it is written in Your Word, through Your Son, Jesus. I am thankful that _____ will recognize the traps of the devil and will be delivered to salvation through the purity of Your Son. You have given _____ the grace and the strength to walk the narrow pathway to Your Kingdom.

I pray that just as Jesus increased in wisdom and stature, You would bless this child with the same wisdom and pour out Your favor and wisdom openly to him/her.

I praise You in advance for _____'s future spouse. Father, Your Word declares that you desire for children to be pure and honorable, waiting upon marriage. I speak blessings to the future union and believe that _____ will be well suited to his/her partner and their household will be in godly order, holding fast to the love of Jesus Christ. Continue to prepare _____ to be the man/woman of God that You desire him/her to be.

_____ shall be diligent and hard-working, never being lazy or undisciplined. Your Word promises great blessing to his/her house and he/she shall always be satisfied and will always increase. Godliness is profitable unto his/her house, and _____ shall receive the promise of life and all that is to come.

Father, thank You for protecting and guiding my child.

In Jesus' name I pray, amen.

Scripture References

Psalm 127:3

Isaiah 54:13

Isaiah 55:11

Proverbs 22:6

1 Peter 5:7

Ephesians 6:4

Deuteronomy 6:7

2 Corinthians 12:9

Ephesians 6:1-3

2 Timothy 1:12

Proverbs 8:17,32

Luke 19:10

Matthew 9:38

2 Corinthians 2:11

2 Timothy 2:26

Job 22:30

Matthew 7:14

Luke 2:52

Hebrews 13:4

1 Thessalonians 4:3

Ephesians 5:22-25

2 Timothy 1:13

Proverbs 13:11

Proverbs 20:13

Romans 12:11

1 Timothy 4:8

1 John 3:8

John 10:10

Matthew 18:18

John 14:13

Psalm 91:1,11

❧ Forty-One ❧

Prayer for a Teenager

Father, in the name of Jesus, I affirm Your Word over my son/daughter. I commit _____ to You and delight myself also in You. I thank You that You deliver _____ out of rebellion into right relationship with us, his/her parents.

Father, the first commandment with a promise is to the child who obeys his/her parents in the Lord. You said that all will be well with him/her and he/she will live long on the earth. I affirm this promise on behalf of my child asking You to give _____ an obedient spirit that he/she may honor (esteem and value as precious) his/her father and mother.

Father, forgive me for mistakes made out of my own unresolved hurts or selfishness which may have caused _____ hurt. I release the anointing that is upon Jesus to bind up and heal our (parents' and child's) broken hearts. Give us the ability to understand and forgive one another as God for Christ's sake has forgiven us. Thank You for the Holy Spirit Who leads us into all truth and corrects erroneous perceptions about past or present situations.

Thank You for teaching us to listen to each other and giving _____ an ear that hears admonition for then he/she will be called wise. I affirm that I will speak excellent and princely things and the opening of my lips shall be for right things. Father, I commit to train and teach _____ in the way that he/she is to go and when _____ is old he/she will not depart from sound doctrine and teaching, but will follow it all the days of his/her life. In the name of Jesus, I command rebellion to be far from the heart of my child and confess that he/she is willing and obedient, free to enjoy the reward of Your promises. _____ shall be peaceful bringing peace to others.

Father, according to Your Word we have been given the ministry of reconciliation and I release this ministry and the word of reconciliation into this family situation. I refuse to provoke or irritate or fret my child, I will not be hard on him/her lest he/she becomes discouraged, feeling inferior and frustrated. I will not break his/her spirit in the name of Jesus and by the power of the Holy Spirit. Father, I forgive my child for the wrongs which he/she has done and thank You that he/she comes to his/her senses and escapes out of the snare of the enemy (rebellion). Thank You for watching over Your Word to perform it, turning and reconciling the heart of the child to the parents and the hearts of the parents to the child. Thank You for bringing my child into a healthy relationship with You and with me that our lives might glorify You! Amen.

Scripture References

Psalm 55:12-14	Proverbs 8:6,7
1 Peter 5:7	Proverbs 22:6
Psalm 37:4	Isaiah 1:19
John 14:6	Isaiah 54:13
Ephesians 6:1-3	2 Corinthians 5:18,19
1 John 1:9	Colossians 3:21
Isaiah 61:1	John 20:23
John 16:13	Ezekial 22:30
Proverbs 15:31	Jeremiah 1:12
Proverbs 13:1	Malachi 4:6

∽ Forty-Two ∾

Children at School

Father, in Jesus' name, I confess Your Word this day concerning my children as they pursue their education and training at school. You are effectually at work in them creating within them the power and desire to please You. They are the head and not the tail, above and not beneath.

I pray that my children will find favor, good understanding and high esteem in the sight of God and their teachers and classmates. I ask You to give my children wisdom and understanding as knowledge is presented to them in all fields of study and endeavor.

137

Father, thank You for giving my children an appreciation for education and helping them to understand that the Source and beginning of all knowledge is You. They have the appetite of the diligent and they are abundantly supplied with educational resources, and their thoughts are those of the steadily diligent which tend only to achievement. Thank You that they are growing in wisdom and knowledge. I will not cease to pray for them, asking that they be filled with the knowledge of Your will bearing fruit in every good work.

Father, I thank You that my children have divine protection since they dwell in the secret place of the Most High. My children trust and find their refuge in You and stand rooted and grounded in Your love. They shall not be led astray by philosophies of men and teaching that is contrary to Truth. You are their shield and buckler protecting them from attacks or threats. Thank You for the angels which You have assigned to them to accompany, defend and preserve them in all their ways of obedience and service. My children are established in Your love which drives all fear out of doors.

I pray that the teachers of my children will be godly men and women of integrity. Give our teachers understanding hearts and wisdom in order that they may walk in the ways of piety and virtue, revering Your holy name. Amen.

138

Scripture References

Philippians 2:13	Psalm 91:1,2
Deuteronomy 28:1,2,13	Ephesians 4:14
Proverbs 3:4	Psalm 91:3-11
1 Kings 4:29	Ephesians 1:17
Daniel 1:4	Psalm 112:8
Proverbs 1:4,7	Ephesians 3:17
Proverbs 3:13	Matthew 18:18
Proverbs 4:5	James 1:5
Colossians 1:9,10	

∽ Forty-Three ∾

The Home

Father, I thank You that You have blessed me with all spiritual blessings in Christ Jesus.

Through skillful and godly wisdom is my house (my life, my home, my family) built, and by understanding it is established on a sound and good foundation. And by knowledge shall the chambers (of its every area) be filled with all precious and pleasant riches — great priceless treasure. The house of the uncompromisingly righteous shall stand. Prosperity and welfare are in my house in the name of Jesus.

My house is securely built. It is founded on a rock — revelation knowledge of Your Word, Father. Jesus is my Cornerstone. Jesus is Lord of my household. Jesus is our Lord — spirit, soul, and body.

Whatever may be our task, we work at it heartily as something done for You, Lord, and not for men. We love each other with the God kind of love, and we dwell in peace. My home is deposited into Your charge, entrusted to Your protection and care.

Father, as for me and my house we shall serve the Lord in Jesus' name. Hallelujah! Amen.

139

Scripture References

Ephesians 1:3

Proverbs 24:3,4 AMP

Proverbs 15:6

Proverbs 12:7 AMP

Psalm 112:3

Luke 6:48

Acts 4:11

Acts 16:31

Philippians 2:10,11

Colossians 3:23

Colossians 3:14,15

Acts 20:32

Joshua 24:15

✍ *Forty-Four* ✍

Complete in Him as a Single

Father, we thank You that _____ desires and earnestly seeks first after the things of Your Kingdom. We thank You that he/she knows that You love him/her and that he/she can trust Your Word.

For in Jesus the whole fullness of Diety (the Godhead) continues to dwell in bodily form — giving complete expression of the Divine Nature, and _____ is in Him and has come to the fullness of life in Christ. He/she is filled with the Godhead — Father, Son, and Holy Spirit — and he/she reaches full spiritual stature. And Christ is the head of all rule and authority — of every angelic principality and power.

So because of Jesus, _____ is complete; Jesus is his/her Lord. He/she comes before You, Father, desiring a born-again Christian mate. We petition that Your will be done in his/her life. Now we enter into that blessed rest by adhering, trusting in, and relying on You, in the name of Jesus. Amen.

141

Scripture References (AMP)

Colossians 2:9,10   Hebrews 4:10

Part III

Prayers for Careers

⊸ Forty-Five ⊷

Beginning Each Day

Father, as the _____ (*owner, president, chairman, manager, supervisor*) of _____ (*name of company*), I come before You rejoicing, for this is the day which You have made and I will be glad in it. To obey is better than sacrifice, so I am making a decision to submit to Your will today that my plans and purposes may be conducted in a manner that will bring honor and glory to You. Cause me to be spiritually and mentally alert in this time of meditation and prayer.

It is into Your keeping that I place my family — my parents, spouse, children and grandchildren — knowing that You are able to keep that which I commit to You against that day. Thank You for the angels that You have commanded concerning me and my family to guard us in all our ways; they will lift us up in their hands so that we will not strike our foot against a stone.

Thank You, Lord, for the tremendous success that my associates and I have experienced in our organization and for the increase in profits and productivity we have enjoyed. Thank You for continuing to influence every person in this business and every decision that is made. Thank You for Your faithfulness to us day by day and for helping us to become all that You desire us to be.

Thank You, Father, for helping to make us a company that continues to grow and expand. We recognize that without Your help, it would not be possible. Without Your direction and guidance, we would be failures; with it we can prosper and have good success. I continue to thank You for the many blessings that You have poured out upon us all.

I especially thank You for the co-laborers with whom I will be interacting today. Give me words of wisdom, words of grace, that I might encourage them and build them up.

Father, I kneel before you, from Whom Your whole family in heaven and on earth derives its name. I pray that out of Your glorious riches You may strengthen each one with power through Your Spirit in his inner being, so that Christ may dwell in each heart through faith.

Now to Him Who is able to do immeasurably more than all we ask or imagine, according to His power that is at work within us, to Him be the glory in this company and in Christ Jesus throughout all generations, for ever and ever! In Jesus' name I pray. Amen.

146

Scripture References

Psalm 118:24

1 Samuel 15:22

2 Timothy 1:12

Psalm 91:11,12 NIV

Lamentations 3:22,23

Joshua 1:8

Ephesians 3:14-17 NIV

Ephesians 3:20 NIV

✎ Forty-Six ✎

Being Equipped for Success

Father, I thank You that the entrance of Your words gives light. I thank You that Your Word which You speak *(and which I speak)* is alive and full of power [making it active, operative, energizing and effective].

I thank You, Father, that [You have given me a spirit] of power and of love and of a calm and well-balanced mind and discipline and self-control. I have Your power and ability and sufficiency, for You have qualified me [making me to be fit and worthy and sufficient] as a minister and dispenser of a new covenant [of salvation through Christ].

In the name of Jesus, I walk out of the realm of failure into the arena of success, giving thanks to You, Father, for You have qualified and made me fit to share the portion which is the inheritance of the saints (Your holy people) in the Light.

Father, You have delivered and drawn me to Yourself out of the control and the dominion of darkness *(failure, doubt and fear)* and have transferred me into the Kingdom of the Son of Your love.

I praise God, the Father of my Lord Jesus Christ, Who has blessed me with every blessing in heaven because I belong to Christ. Your divine power has given me everything I need for life and godliness through my knowledge of Him Who called me by His own glory and goodness. I rejoice in Jesus Who has come that I might have life and have it more abundantly.

I am a new creation, for I am (ingrafted) in Christ, the Messiah. The old [previous moral and spiritual condition] has passed away. Behold, the fresh and new has come! I forget those things which are behind me and reach forth unto those things which are before me. I am crucified with Christ: nevertheless I live; yet not I, but Christ lives in me: and the life which I now live in the flesh I live by the faith of the Son of God, Who loved me, and gave Himself for me.

149

Father, I attend to Your Word. I consent and submit to Your sayings. Your words shall not depart from my sight; I will keep them in the center of my heart. For they are life *(success)* to me, healing and health to all my flesh. I keep and guard my heart with all vigilance and above all that I guard, for out of it flow the springs of life.

I will not let mercy and kindness and truth forsake me. I bind them about my neck; I write them upon the tablet of my heart. So therefore I will find favor, good understanding and high esteem in the sight [or judgment] of God and man.

Father, my delight and desire are in Your Law, and on it I habitually meditate (ponder and study) by day and by night. Therefore I am like a tree firmly planted [and tended] by the streams of water, ready to bring forth my fruit in my season; my leaf also shall not fade or wither, and everything I do shall prosper [and come to maturity].

Now thanks be unto God, which always causeth us to triumph in Christ!

In Jesus' name I pray, amen.

Scripture References

Psalm 119:130

Hebrews 4:12 AMP

2 Timothy 1:7 AMP

2 Corinthians 3:5 AMP

Colossians 1:12,13 AMP

Ephesians 1:3 TLB

2 Peter 1:3 NIV

John 10:10 AMP

2 Corinthians 5:17 AMP

Philippians 3:13

Galatians 2:20

Proverbs 4:20-23 AMP

Proverbs 3:3,4 AMP

Psalm 1:2,3 AMP

2 Corinthians 2:14

Forty-Seven

Assuring the Success of a Business

Father, I come before You with thanksgiving. You have qualified and made me fit to share the portion which is the inheritance of the saints (Your holy people) in the Light. You have delivered me out of the power of darkness and translated me into the Kingdom of Your dear Son.

As I know You better, You will give me, through Your great power, everything I need for living a truly good life: You even share Your own glory and Your own goodness with me! And by that same mighty power You have given me all the other rich and wonderful blessings You promised; for instance, the promise to save me from the lust and rottenness all around me, and to give me Your own character.

You have delivered me out of the power of darkness and translated me into the Kingdom of Your dear Son.

Where Your Word is, there is light and understanding. Your Word does not return to You void, but it always accomplishes what it is sent to do.

I am a joint-heir with Jesus, and as Your son/daughter, I accept that the communication of my faith is effectual by the acknowledging of every good thing which is in me in Christ Jesus.

Father, I commit my works (the plans and cares of my business) to You, trusting them wholly to You. Since You are effectually at work in me [You cause my thoughts to become agreeable with Your will] so that my (business) plans shall be established and succeed.

In the name of Jesus, I submit to every kind of wisdom and understanding (practical insight and prudence) which You have lavished upon me in accordance with the riches and generosity of Your gracious favor.

Father, I affirm that I obey Your Word by making an honest living with my own hands so that I may be able to give to those in need. In Your strength and according to Your grace I provide for myself and my own family.

Thank You, Father, for making all grace (every favor and earthly blessing) come to me in abundance, so that I, having all sufficiency in all things, may abound to every good work.

Father, thank You for the ministering spirits that You have assigned to go forth to minister on my behalf and bring in trade. Jesus said that those who put their faith and trust in Him are the light of the world. In His name my light shall so shine before all men that they may see my good works and glorify You, my heavenly Father.

152

Thank You for the grace to remain diligent in seeking knowledge and skill in areas in which I am inexperienced. I ask You for wisdom and the ability to understand righteousness, justice and fair dealing [in every area and relationship]. I affirm that I am faithful and committed to Your Word. My life and business are founded upon its principles.

Thank You, Father, for the success of my business!
In Jesus' name I pray, amen.

Scripture References

Colossians 1:12 AMP	*Ephesians 4:28 AMP*
Colossians 1:13	*1 Timothy 5:8 AMP*
2 Peter 1:3-5 TLB	*2 Corinthians 9:8 AMP*
Psalm 119:130	*2 Corinthians 9:8*
Isaiah 55:11	*Hebrews 1:14*
2 Corinthians 6:16,18	*Matthew 5:14,16*
Philemon 6	*Proverbs 22:29 AMP*
Proverbs 16:3 AMP	*Proverbs 2:9 AMP*
Philippians 2:13 AMP	*Proverbs 4:20-22 AMP*
Ephesians 1:7,8 AMP	

153

∽ *Forty-Eight* ∾

Making a Difficult Decision

Father, I bring this decision before You. It is a difficult one for me to make in the natural, but I know that with You it can be an easy one.

I ask You, Lord, to help me see both sides of this issue and to consider all the facts involved in it. Help me to properly evaluate both the positive and negative attributes of this situation.

Lord, I recognize that an important part of being an excellent manager is decisiveness. In processing the information and considering the possible repercussions or benefits of this decision, help me to avoid the paralysis of analysis. Help me to get the information I need and to evaluate it carefully and wisely.

Help me, Father, to hear Your voice, and so to make the right and correct decision in this case. Keep me from acting in haste but also from delaying too long to reach a decision.

Father, help me not to be influenced by my own personal wants or desires concerning this matter under consideration. Instead, help me to perceive and choose what is best for my department or company, regardless of how I may feel about it personally. Help me to undertake and carry out this decision-making process accurately and objectively.

Thank You for Your guidance and direction in this situation.

In Jesus' name I pray, amen.

Scripture References

Isaiah 11:2 AMP   John 10:27

Colossians 4:1 NIV   Philippians 2:3 NIV

Proverbs 28:1   Judges 6:12

↶ Forty-Nine ↷

Prayer for the Company

Father, I pray for _____ today. I thank You for this organization and for the opportunity to be a part of it. I am grateful for the chance to earn the income this firm provides for me and my family and for the blessing that it has been to me and all its employees.

Father, I thank You that _____ enjoys a good reputation, that it is seen well in the minds of its customers and vendors. Thank You that it prospers and makes a profit, that You give it favor with its clients, that You continue to provide wisdom and insight to those within it who occupy important decision-making positions.

It is my prayer that _____ will continue to thrive and prosper. Thank You for increased sales and expanded markets.

Thank You, Father, for the creativity that is evident in the different areas of the company — new product ideas and new servicing concepts — innovations and techniques that keep this organization vibrant, alive and thriving.

156

I ask You, Lord, to bless it and to cause it to be a blessing to the market it serves, as well as to all those whose lives are invested in it on a daily basis.

In Jesus' name I pray, amen.

Scripture References

1 Timothy 2:1-3	Proverbs 3:21
3 John 2	Psalm 115:14
Joshua 1:8	Proverbs 8:12
Psalm 5:12	Malachi 3:12 AMP
Proverbs 2:7	Hebrews 6:14

Fifty

Prayer for a Superior

Father, in Your Word, You said to pray for those who exercise authority over us, so I pray for my manager/supervisor today. I ask You to give him/her clarity of thought concerning every decision made this day. Help him/her to clearly identify and accurately assess every potential problem. Help him/her to make the right decisions — to respond, and not to react, to whatever situation or circumstance might arise during the course of the day.

I ask You, Father, to help him/her to set the proper priorities today. Reveal to him/her what tasks are most important and cause him/her to inspire us to perform our duties to the best of our abilities.

I ask that You help him/her to be sensitive to the needs of those under his/her supervision, those who work for him/her. Help him/her to realize that not everyone is the same and that no two people respond or react in the same way. Help him/her to adapt his/her management style or technique to the strengths, weaknesses and personality type of each individual. Grant him/her the ability to manage beyond his/her own natural gifts and talents. I pray that he/she will rely upon You, drawing strength, wisdom and insight from You.

I purpose in my heart to set a guard over my mouth. I refuse to say anything negative or disrespectful about my manager/ supervisor. I choose to support him/her and to say only good things about him/her.

Lord, I ask You to give him/her a peaceful spirit, so that even in the midst of great turmoil he/she may act with surety and confidence and make wise decisions. Help me to be sensitive to his/her needs and responsibilities. Show me ways, Lord, to support him/her and to assist him/her in the performance of his/her duties.

Father, You have said in Your Word that Your Spirit will show us things to come. I ask You to show my manager/supervisor the solution to small problems before they become major problems. Grant him/her creative ideas on how he/she can better lead and manage his/her department.

For all these things I give You thanks, praise and glory, in Jesus' name. Amen.

Scripture References

1 Timothy 2:1-3 AMP	Isaiah 40:29-31 AMP
1 Corinthians 2:16	Philippians 4:7
Ephesians 4:23,24	Hebrews 12:14
Matthew 6:33 AMP	John 14:26
Romans 12:10	John 16:13

~ *Fifty-One* ~

Prayer When Persecuted at Work

Father, I come to You in the name that is above all other names — the name of Jesus. Your name is a strong tower that I can run into and be safe when I am persecuted on the job.

Lord, I admit that these unkind words really hurt me. I desire to be accepted by my boss and co-workers, but I long to obey You and follow Your commandments. I know that Jesus was tempted just as I am, but He didn't give in to sin or hate. Please give me Your mercy and grace to deal with this situation. I look to You for my comfort; You are a true Friend at all times.

Thank You, Lord, for never leaving me alone or rejecting me. I make a decision to forgive the people who have spoken unkind words about me. I ask You to work this forgiveness in my heart. I submit to You and reject the disappointment and anger that have attempted to consume me. Specifically right now I forgive _____.

160

I ask You to cause this situation to accommodate itself for good in my life. **To you, O Lord, I lift up my soul; in you I trust, O my God. Do not let me be put to shame, nor let my enemies triumph over me** (Ps. 25:1,2 NIV). Because I love You, O Lord, You will rescue me; You will protect me because I acknowledge Your name. I will call upon You, and You will deliver me; You will be with me in trouble, You will deliver me and honor me.

Father, I will resist the temptation to strike back in anger. I purpose to love _____ with the love of Jesus in me. Mercy and truth are written upon the tablets of my heart; therefore, You will cause me to find favor and understanding with my boss and co-workers. Keep me from self-righteousness so that I may walk in Your righteousness. Thank You for sending and giving me friends who will stand by me and teach me how to guard my heart with all diligence.

161

I declare that in the midst of all these things I am more than a conqueror through Jesus Who loves me. I can use the witty inventions You have provided me, and I will be confident in Your wisdom when working. I am of good courage and pray that freedom of utterance be given to me as I do my job.

In Jesus' name I pray, amen.

Scripture References

Philippians 2:9

Proverbs 18:10

Hebrews 4:15

Proverbs 17:17

Hebrews 13:5

Proverbs 16:4 AMP

Psalm 91:14,15 NIV

Proverbs 3:3,4

Proverbs 4:23

Romans 8:37

Proverbs 8:12

Psalm 31:24

Ephesians 6:19

∽ Fifty-Two ∾

Improving Harmony and Cooperation

Devotional Reading

Fill up and complete my joy by living in harmony and being of the same mind and one in purpose, having the same love, being in full accord and of one harmonious mind and intention.

Philippians 2:2 AMP

163

Prayer

Father, Jesus prayed that His followers would be one. I enter into agreement with my Lord, praying for the development of harmony and cooperation among the leadership and employees of _____ (*company name*). I ask for wisdom to know how to resolve any conflicts that may have arisen among the departments.

As _____ (*president, supervisor, manager, etc.*) of _____ I institute the principles of peace, uprooting and dissolving confusion, rivalries, arguments, and disagreements for the good of our company _____ and the welfare of all concerned.

In the name of Jesus I submit myself to You, Father, and resist the devil. I overcome the fear of confrontation (and its outcome) and initiate resolution. I desire to pursue peace with my co-workers, customers, family and friends.

Give me the courage to go to anyone who is holding anything against me that we might be reconciled. Then I will come and offer my gift to You.

Also, I ask for the boldness of the Lion of Judah to go to anyone who has sinned against me and _____ *(company name)*, confronting his/her fault without attacking him/her. I am requesting and believing for reconciliation. Help me to forgive even if he/she refuses to be reconciled and follow through with the necessary steps for his/her good and the company's welfare.

164

Thank You for the harmony and cooperation necessary to accomplish our common goals.

Glory be to You Who by Your mighty power at work within us is able to do far more than we would ever dare to ask or even dream of — infinitely beyond our highest prayers, desires, thoughts or hopes. May You be given glory forever and ever through endless ages because of Your master plan of salvation for the Church through Jesus Christ.

In Jesus' name I pray, amen.

Scripture References

John 17:21

James 1:5

James 4:7

Hebrews 12:14 NKJV

Matthew 5:23,24

Matthew 18:15

Ephesians 3:20,21 TLB

Fifty-Three

Overcoming Negative Work Attitudes

Thank You, Father, for watching over Your Word to perform it as I speak it over myself and those who work with me in Your service, especially _____. I say that he/she is obedient to his/her employers — bosses or supervisors — having respect for them and being eager to please them, in singleness of motive and with all his/her heart, as [service] to Christ [Himself]. Not in the way of eye-service [as if they were watching him/her] but as a servant (employee) of Christ, doing Your will heartily and with his/her whole soul.

_____ readily renders service with goodwill, as to You and not to men. He/she knows that for whatever good he/she does, he/she will receive his/her reward from You.

_____ does all things without grumbling and faultfinding and complaining [against You] and questioning and doubting [within himself/herself]. He/she is blameless and guileless, Your child, without blemish (faultless, unrebukable) in the midst of a crooked and wicked generation [spiritually perverted and perverse], among whom he/she is seen as a bright light (a star or beacon shining out clearly) in the [dark] world.

_____ reveres You, Lord, and his/her work is a sincere expression of his/her devotion to You. Whatever may be his/her task, he/she works at it heartily (from the soul), as something done for You, knowing that [The One Whom] he/she is actually serving [is] the Lord Christ (the Messiah).

In His name I pray, amen.

Scripture References (AMP)

| Jeremiah 12:1 | Philippians 2:14,15 |
| Ephesians 6:5-8 | Colossians 3:22-24 |

167

✑ Fifty-Four ✑

Prayer for an Increase in Personal Productivity

Father, I come to You out of frustration because I am not pleased with my performance on the job. It seems that I am not producing that which I should be producing because I am just not as efficient or effective as I need to be.

Lord, I ask for Your help in planning my day, paying attention to my duties, staying focused on my assignment, establishing priorities in my work and making steady progress toward my objectives.

Give me insight, Father. Help me to see any habits that I may have that might tend to make me non-productive. Reveal to me ways to better handle the tedious tasks I must perform so that I can achieve the greatest results possible. Help me to organize my efforts, schedule my activities and budget my time.

From books, by Your Spirit, through the people who work with me or by whatever means You choose, Lord, reveal to me that which I need to know and do in order to become a more productive, fruitful worker.

My heart's desire is to give my very best to You and to my employer. When I become frustrated because that is not taking place, help me, Father, by the power of Your Spirit to do whatever is necessary to correct that situation so that I can once again function with accuracy and proficiency.

Thank you, Lord, for bringing all these things to pass in my life.

In Jesus' name I pray, amen.

Scripture References

Psalm 118:24

Proverbs 16:9 AMP

Proverbs 19:21 AMP

Ephesians 1:17

Psalm 119:99 AMP

Proverbs 9:10 AMP

1 Corinthians 4:5

↜ Fifty-Five ↝

Undertaking a
New Project

Lord, I lift up to You this new project which we are considering. I feel that it is one we should be a part of, something we should do, but I seek Your wisdom concerning it.

If it is not of You, Lord, please put a check in our spirits. Direct us to stop planning and working on it and to put a halt to any further waste of time and energy.

If it is of You, Father, then I thank You for Your counsel and assistance concerning it. Give us understanding and discernment in the preparation stages as we gather the information we need to devise a course of action and to plan the budget for the work. Help us to accumulate the facts and figures we need to carry out this plan in accordance with Your will and purpose.

Thank You, Lord, for Your insight and wisdom. I ask You to give each of us guidance and direction by Your Holy Spirit so we will know how to assimilate the information we gather and use it to maximum advantage. Reveal to us any hidden

170

costs or expenses so that we can take them into account in preparing an accurate budget and detailed forecast of both time and money.

Give all of us involved in this project the ability to concentrate our attention and focus our efforts so that we can successfully complete this undertaking and thereby bring honor and glory to You through it.

In Jesus' name I pray, amen.

Scripture References

Proverbs 8:12 AMP   Ephesians 1:8,9,17 AMP
Isaiah 11:2 NIV   Luke 12:2 NIV
Jeremiah 29:11-13   Romans 12:2 NIV
Jeremiah 33:3 NIV

171

～ Fifty-Six ～

Conducting a Meeting

Father, in the name of Jesus, may Your wisdom prevail today in our meeting. Help each of us to be quick to listen, slow to speak and slow to become angry, for man's anger does not bring about the righteous life that You desire.

Lord, I recognize Your Holy Spirit and welcome Him to the meeting, acknowledging our dependence upon His presence and guidance. With His help, I purpose to respect and regard every individual's opinions as valuable and worthy of consideration. Knowing that a soft answer turns away wrath, I will be polite and courteous in all our deliberations.

Help each one of us to offer our opinions at the appropriate time and to resist any feelings of self-pity or self-aggrandizement. Guard us from thinking that our opinions are not being heard.

I pray for those who have to deal with rejection. Help them to know that any negation of their opinions or suggestions is not personal.

Should my own opinions be rejected, I refuse to believe that I, personally, am rejected. I will remember that my opinions are not me.

Father, Your love in me does not insist on its own rights or its own way, for it is not self-seeking. I submit to the wisdom that comes from heaven for it is pure, peace loving, considerate, full of mercy and good fruit, impartial and sincere. As a peacemaker, I sow in peace, reaping a harvest of righteousness.

Thank You, Father, for wisdom that is from above. In Jesus' name I pray, amen.

Scripture References

Ephesians 1:17

James 1:19,20 NIV

John 16:13

Proverbs 15:1

1 Peter 5:5 NIV

Romans 12:10 NIV

1 Corinthians 13:5 AMP

James 3:17,18 NIV

173

Part IV

Prayers for Ministry

❧ Fifty-Seven ❧

The Body of Christ

Father, we pray and confess Your Word over the Body of Christ. We pray that Your people be filled with the full, deep, and clear knowledge of Your will in all spiritual things. We pray they live and conduct themselves in a manner worthy of You, Lord, fully pleasing to You and desiring to please You in all things, bearing fruit in every good work, and steadily growing and increasing in and by the knowledge of You, with fuller, deeper, and clearer insight.

We pray that the Body of Christ will be invigorated and strengthened with all power, according to the might of Your glory, to exercise every kind of endurance and patience with joy, giving thanks to You, Father, Who has qualified and made them fit to share the portion which is the inheritance of the saints (God's holy people) in the Light. You, Father, have delivered and drawn them to Yourself out of the control and the dominion of darkness and have transferred them into the Kingdom of the Son of Your love, in Whom they have their redemption through His blood, which means the remission of their sins.

177

Father, You delight at the sight of the Body of Christ, standing shoulder to shoulder in such orderly array and the firmness and the solid front and steadfastness of their faith in Christ, leaning on Him in absolute trust and confidence in His power, wisdom, and goodness. They walk — regulate their lives and conduct themselves — in union with and conformity to Him, having the roots of their being firmly and deeply planted in Him, being continually built up in Him, becoming increasingly more confirmed and established in the faith.

Your people, Father, clothe themselves as Your own picked representatives — Your chosen ones, who are purified and holy and well-beloved by You — by putting on behavior marked by tender-hearted pity and mercy, kind feeling, gentle ways, and patience. They have the power to endure whatever comes, with good temper. They are gentle and forbearing with each other and, if they have a grievance or complaint against another, readily pardon each other. As You, Lord, have freely forgiven them, so do they also forgive.

Your people put on love and enfold themselves with the bond of perfectness — which binds everything together completely in ideal harmony. They let the peace from Jesus act as umpire continually in their hearts — deciding and settling with all finality all the questions that arise in their minds — in that peaceful state to which they are called. They are thankful, appreciative, giving praise to You always.

The Body of Christ lets the Word spoken by Christ the Messiah have its home in their hearts and minds. It dwells in them in all richness, as they teach, admonish, and train each other in all insight, intelligence, and wisdom in spiritual songs, making melody to You, Father, with Your grace in their hearts.

And whatever they do in word or deed, they do everything in the name of the Lord Jesus and in dependence upon His person, giving praise to You, Father, through Him!

In Jesus' name, amen.

Scripture References (AMP)

Colossians 1:9-14   Colossians 2:5-7
Colossians 3:12-17

∽ *Fifty-Eight* ∾

Salvation of the Lost

Father, it is written in Your Word, **First of all, then, I admonish and urge that petitions, prayers, intercessions and thanksgivings be offered on behalf of all men** (1 Timothy 2:1 AMP).

Therefore, Father, we bring the lost of the world this day — every man, woman, and child from here to the farthest corner of the earth — before You. As we intercede, we use our faith believing that thousands this day have the opportunity to make Jesus their Lord.

Satan, we bind your blinding spirit of antichrist and loose you from your assignment against those who have that opportunity to make Jesus Lord.

We ask the Lord of the harvest to thrust the perfect laborers across these lives this day to share the good news of the Gospel in a special way so that they will listen and understand it. We believe that they will not be able to resist the wooing of the Holy Spirit, for You, Father, bring them to repentance by Your goodness and love.

We confess that they shall see who have never been told of Jesus. They shall understand who have never heard of Jesus. And they shall come out of the snare of the devil who has held them captive. They shall open their eyes and turn from darkness to light — from the power of Satan to You, God!

In Jesus' name, amen.

Scripture References

1 Timothy 2:1,2 AMP

Matthew 18:18

Matthew 9:38

Romans 2:4

Romans 15:21 AMP

2 Timothy 2:26 AMP

∿ Fifty-Nine ∿

Vision for a Church

Father, in the name of Jesus, we come into Your presence thanking You for _____(name of church). You have called us to be saints in _____(name of city) and around the world. As we lift our voices in one accord, we recognize that You are God, and everything was made by and for You. We call into being those things that be not as though they were.

We thank You that we all speak the same thing: there is no division among us; we are perfectly joined together in the same mind. Grant unto us, Your representatives here, a boldness to speak Your Word which You will confirm with signs following. We thank You that we have workmen in abundance and all manner of cunning people for every manner of work. Each department operates in the excellence of ministry and intercessions. We have in our church the ministry gifts for the edifying of this body till we all come into the unity of the faith, and the knowledge of the Son of God, unto a mature person. None of our people will be children, tossed to and fro, and carried about with every wind of doctrine. We speak the truth in love.

We are a growing and witnessing body of believers becoming _____(number) strong.

We have every need met. Therefore, we meet the needs of people who come — spirit, soul, and body. We ask for the wisdom of God in meeting these needs. Father, we thank You for the ministry facilities that will more than meet the needs of the ministry You have called us to. Our church is prospering financially, and we have more than enough to meet every situation. We have everything we need to carry out Your Great Commission and reach the _____(name of city or country) area for Jesus. We are a people of love as love is shed abroad in our hearts by the Holy Spirit. We thank You that the Word of God is living big in all of us and Jesus is Lord!

We are a supernatural church, composed of supernatural people doing supernatural things, for we are laborers together with God. We thank You for Your presence among us and we lift our hands and praise Your holy name! Amen.

Scripture References

Acts 4:24	Ephesians 4:11-15
Romans 4:17	Philippians 4:19
1 Corinthians 1:10	Romans 5:5
Acts 4:29	1 Corinthians 3:9
Mark 16:20b	Psalm 63:4
Exodus 35:33	

This prayer was written by and used with the permission of T. R. King; Valley Christian Center; Roanoke, Virginia.

⌒ Sixty ⌒

Ministers

Father, in the name of Jesus, we pray and confess that the Spirit of the Lord shall rest upon _____...the spirit of wisdom and understanding, the spirit of counsel and might, the spirit of knowledge. We pray that as Your Spirit rests upon _____ He will make him/her of quick understanding because You, Lord, have anointed and qualified him/her to preach the Gospel to the meek, the poor, the wealthy, the afflicted. You have sent _____ to bind up and heal the brokenhearted, to proclaim liberty to the physical and spiritual captives, and the opening of the prison and of the eyes to those who are bound.

_____ shall be called the priest of the Lord. People will speak of him/her as a minister of God. He/she shall eat the wealth of the nations.

We pray and believe that no weapon that is formed against _____ shall prosper and that any tongue that rises against him/her in judgment shall be shown to be in the wrong. We pray that You prosper _____ abundantly, Lord — physically, spiritually, and financially.

We confess that _____ holds fast and follows the pattern of wholesome and sound teaching in all faith and love which is for us in Christ Jesus. _____ guards and keeps with the greatest love the precious and excellently adapted Truth which has been entrusted to him/her by the Holy Spirit Who makes His home in _____.

Lord, we pray and believe that, each and every day, freedom of utterance is given _____, that he/she will open his/her mouth boldly and courageously as he/she ought to do to get the Gospel to the people. Thank You, Lord, for the added strength which comes superhumanly that You have given him/her.

We hereby confess that we shall stand behind _____ and undergird him/her in prayer. We will say only that good thing that will edify _____. We will not allow ourselves to judge him/her, but will continue to intercede for him/her and speak and pray blessings upon him/her in the name of Jesus. Thank You, Jesus, for the answers. Hallelujah! Amen.

185

Scripture References

Isaiah 11:2,3	*2 Timothy 1:13,14 AMP*
Isaiah 61:1,6 AMP	*Ephesians 6:19,20 AMP*
Isaiah 54:17 AMP	*1 Peter 3:12*

Sixty-One

Missionaries

Father, we lift before You those in the Body of Christ who are out in the field carrying the good news of the Gospel — not only in this country but also around the world. We lift those in the Body of Christ who are suffering persecution — those who are in prison for their beliefs. Father, we know that You watch over Your Word to perform it, that Your Word prospers in the thing for which You sent it. Therefore, we speak Your Word and establish Your covenant on this earth. We pray here and others receive the answer there by the Holy Spirit.

186

Thank You, Father, for revealing unto Your people the integrity of Your Word and that they must be firm in faith against the devil's onset, withstanding him. Father, You are their light, salvation, refuge, and stronghold. You hide them in Your shelter and set them high upon a rock. It is Your will that each one prospers, is in good health, and lives in victory. You set the prisoners free, feed the hungry, execute justice, rescue, and deliver.

In Jesus' name, we bind you, Satan, and every menacing spirit that would stir up against God's people.

We commission the ministering spirits to go forth and provide the necessary help for and assistance to these heirs of salvation. We and they are strong in the Lord and in the power of Your might, quenching every dart of the devil in Jesus' name.

Father, we use our faith covering these in the Body of Christ with Your Word. We say that no weapon formed against them shall prosper, and any tongue that rises against them in judgment they shall show to be in the wrong. This peace, security, and triumph over opposition is their inheritance as Your children. This is the righteousness which they obtain from You, Father, which You impart to them as their justification. They are far from even the thought of destruction, for they shall not fear and terror shall not come near them.

Father, You say You will establish them to the end — keep them steadfast, give them strength, and guarantee their vindication, that is, be their warrant against all accusation or indictment. They are not anxious beforehand how they shall reply in defense or what they are to say, for the Holy Spirit teaches them in that very hour and moment what they ought to say to those in the outside world, their speech being seasoned with salt.

We commit these our brothers and sisters in the Lord to You, Father, deposited into Your charge, entrusting them to Your protection and care, for You are faithful. You strengthen them and set them on a firm foundation and guard them from the evil one. We join our voices in praise unto You, Most High, that You might silence the enemy and avenger. Praise the Lord! Greater is He who is in us than he who is in the world!

In His name we pray, amen.

Scripture References

Jeremiah 1:12

Isaiah 55:11

1 Peter 5:9

Psalm 27:1,5

3 John 2

1 John 5:4,5

Psalm 146:7

Psalm 144:7

Matthew 18:18

Hebrews 1:14

Ephesians 6:10,16

Isaiah 54:14,17

1 Corinthians 1:8

Luke 12:11,12

Colossians 4:6

Acts 20:32

2 Thessalonians 3:3

Psalm 8:2

1 John 4:4

∽ Sixty-Two ∾

Revival

Father, in the name of Jesus, You have revived us again that Your people may rejoice in You. Thank You for showing us Your mercy and lovingkindness, O Lord, and for granting us Your salvation. You have created in us a clean heart, O God, and renewed a right, persevering and steadfast spirit within us. You have restored unto us the joy of Your salvation, and You are upholding us with a willing spirit. Now we will teach transgressors Your ways, and sinners shall be converted and return to You.

We therefore cleanse our ways by taking heed and keeping watch [on ourselves] according to Your Word [conforming our lives to it]. Since Your [great] promises are ours, we cleanse ourselves from everything that contaminates and defiles our bodies and spirits, and bring [our] consecration to completeness in the (reverential) fear of God. With our whole hearts have we sought You, inquiring for You and of You, and yearning for You; O let us not wander or step aside [either in ignorance or

189

willfully] from Your commandments. Your Word have we laid up in our hearts, that we might not sin against You.

Jesus, thank You for cleansing us through the Word — the teachings — which You have given us. We delight ourselves in Your statutes; we will not forget Your Word. Deal bountifully with Your servants, that we may live; and we will observe Your Word [hearing, receiving, loving, and obeying it].

Father, in the name of Jesus, we are doers of the Word, and not merely listeners to it. It is You, O Most High, Who has revived and stimulated us according to Your Word! Thank You for turning away our eyes from beholding vanity [idols and idolatry]; and restoring us to vigorous life and health in Your ways. Behold, we long for Your precepts; in Your righteousness give us renewed life. This is our comfort and consolation in our affliction, that Your Word has revived us and given us life.

We strip ourselves of our former natures — put off and discard our old unrenewed selves — which characterized our previous manner of life. We are constantly renewed in the spirit of our minds — having a fresh mental and spiritual attitude; and we put on the new nature (the regenerate self) created in God's image, (Godlike) in true righteousness and holiness. Though our outer man is (progressively) decaying and wasting away, our inner self is being

190

(progressively) renewed day after day. Hallelujah! Amen.

Scripture References (AMP)

Psalm 85:6,7

Psalm 51:10,12,13

Psalm 119:9-11

2 Corinthians 7:1

John 15:3

Psalm 119:16,17

James 1:22

Psalm 119:25

Psalm 119:37,40,50

Ephesians 4:22-24

2 Corinthians 4:16b

∾ Sixty-Three ∾

Success of a Conference

Father, we pray that those who hear the messages at the _____ conference will believe — adhere to and trust in and rely on Jesus as the Christ, and that all those You have called to attend the conference will be there and receive what You have for them.

Let it be known and understood by all that it is in the name and through the power and authority of Jesus Christ of Nazareth, and by means of Him that this conference is successful.

The speakers shall be filled with and controlled by the Holy Spirit. When the people see the boldness and unfettered eloquence of the speakers, they shall marvel and recognize that they have been with Jesus. Everybody shall be praising and glorifying God for what shall be occuring. By the hands of the ministers, numerous and startling signs and wonders will be performed among the people.

Father, in the name of Jesus, we thank You that You have observed the enemy's threats and have granted us, Your bondservants, full freedom to declare Your message fearlessly — while You stretch out Your hand to cure and perform signs and wonders through the authority and by the power of the name of Your Holy Child and Servant Jesus.

We thank You, Father, that when we pray, the place in which we are assembled will be shaken; and we shall all be filled with the Holy Spirit, and Your people shall continue to speak the Word of God with freedom and boldness and courage.

By common consent, we shall all meet together at the conference. More and more individuals shall join themselves with us — a crowd of both men and women. The people shall gather from the north, south, east, and west, bringing the sick and those troubled with foul spirits, and they shall all be cured.

Thank You, Father, that our speakers are men and women of good and attested character and repute, full of the Holy Spirit and wisdom. The people who shall hear will not be able to resist the intelligence and the wisdom and the inspiration of the Spirit with which they speak, in the name of Jesus.

Thank You, Father, for the performance of Your Word in the name of Jesus! Amen.

Scripture References (AMP)

Acts 4:10,13,21   Acts 5:12b,13,16

Acts 5:12a   Acts 6:3,10

Acts 4:29-31

193

~ Sixty-Four ~

Protection and Deliverance of a City

Father, in the name of Jesus, we have received Your power — ability, efficiency, and might — because the Holy Spirit has come upon us; and we are Your witnesses in _____ and to the ends — the very bounds — of the earth.

We fearlessly and confidently and boldly draw near to the throne of grace that we may receive mercy and find grace to help in good time for every need — appropriate help and well-timed help, coming just when we in the city of _____ need it.

Father, thank You for sending forth Your commandments to the earth; Your Word runs very swiftly throughout _____. Your Word continues to grow and spread.

Father, we seek — inquire for, require and request — the peace and welfare of _____ in which You have caused us to live. We pray to You for the welfare of this city and do our part by getting involved in it. We will not let [false] prophets and

194

diviners who are in our midst deceive us; we pay no attention and attach no significance to our dreams which we dream, or to theirs. Destroy [their schemes], O Lord; confuse their tongues; for we have seen violence and strife in the city.

Holy Spirit, we ask You to visit our city and open the eyes of the people, that they may turn from darkness to light, and from the power of Satan to God, so that they may thus receive forgiveness and release from their sins and a place and portion among those who are consecrated and purified by faith in Jesus.

Father, we pray for deliverance and salvation for those who are following the course and fashion of this world — who are under the sway of the tendency of this present age — following the prince of the power of the air.

Father, forgive them, for they know not what they do.

195

We speak to the prince of the power of the air, to the god of this world who blinds the unbelievers' minds (that they should not discern the truth), and we command that he leave the heavens above our city.

Thank You, Father, for the guardian angels assigned to this place who war for us in the heavenlies.

In the name of Jesus, we stand victorious over the principalities, powers, rulers of the darkness of this world, and spiritual wickedness in high places over

_____ .

We ask the Holy Spirit to sweep through the gates of our city and convince the people and bring demonstration to them about sin and about righteousness — uprightness of heart and right standing with God — and about judgment.

Father, You said, **For I know the thoughts and plans that I have for you...thoughts and plans for welfare and peace, and not for evil, to give you hope in your final outcome** (Jer. 29:11 AMP). By the blessing of the influence of the upright and God's favor [because of them] the city of _____ is exalted. Amen.

Scripture References

Acts 1:8 AMP

Hebrews 4:16 AMP

Psalm 147:15 AMP

Acts 12:24 AMP

Jeremiah 29:7,8 AMP

Psalm 55:9 AMP

Acts 26:18 AMP

Ephesians 2:2 AMP

Luke 23:34a AMP

2 Corinthians 4:4 AMP

Ephesians 6:12

Psalm 101:8 AMP

John 16:8 AMP

Jeremiah 29:11 AMP

Proverbs 11:11a AMP

∼ Sixty-Five ∼

American Government

Father, in Jesus' name, we give thanks for the United States and its government. We hold up in prayer before You the men and women who are in positions of authority. We pray and intercede for the president, the representatives, the senators, the judges of our land, the policemen and the policewomen, as well as the governors and mayors, and for all those who are in authority over us in any way. We pray that the Spirit of the Lord rests upon them.

We believe that skillful and godly wisdom has entered into the heart of our president and knowledge is pleasant to him. Discretion watches over him; understanding keeps him and delivers him from the way of evil and from evil men.

Father, we ask that You compass the president about with men and women who make their hearts and ears attentive to godly counsel and do that which is right in Your sight. We believe You cause them to be men and women of integrity who are obedient concerning us that we may lead a quiet and peaceable life in all godliness and honesty. We pray that the upright shall dwell in our government...that men and women blameless and complete in Your sight, Father, shall remain in these positions of authority; but the wicked shall be cut off from our government and the treacherous shall be rooted out of it.

Your Word declares that **blessed is the nation whose God is the Lord** (Ps. 33:12). We receive Your blessing. Father, You are our refuge and stronghold in times of trouble (high cost, destitution, and desperation). So we declare with our mouths that Your people dwell safely in this land, and we *prosper* abundantly. We are more than conquerors through Christ Jesus!

It is written in Your Word that the heart of the king is in the hand of the Lord, and you turn it whichever way You desire. We believe the heart of our leader is in Your hand and that his decisions are divinely directed of the Lord.

We give thanks unto You that the good news of the Gospel is published in our land. The Word of the Lord prevails and grows mightily in the hearts and lives of the people. We give thanks for this land and the leaders You have given to us, in Jesus' name.

Jesus is Lord over the United States! Amen.

Scripture References

1 Timothy 2:1-3

Proverbs 2:10-12,21,22

Psalm 33:12

Psalm 9:9

Deuteronomy 28:10,11

Romans 8:37 AMP

Proverbs 21:1

Acts 12:24

⌒ Sixty-Six ⌒

Members of the Armed Forces

Father, our troops have been sent into _____ as peacekeepers. We petition You, Lord, according to Psalm 91, for the safety of our military personnel.

This is no afternoon athletic contest that our armed forces will walk away from and forget about in a couple of hours. This is for keeps, a life-or-death fight to the finish against the devil and all his angels. We look beyond human instruments of conflict and address the forces and authorities and rulers of darkness and powers in the spiritual world. As children of the Most High God we enforce the triumphant victory of our Lord Jesus Christ.

Jesus stripped you, Satan, of your principalities and powers, making a show of you openly. Our Lord and Master defeated you. All power and authority both in heaven and earth belong to Him. Righteousness and truth shall prevail. Nations shall come to the light of the Gospel.

We petition heaven to turn our troops into a real peacekeeping force by pouring out the glory of

God through our men and women in that part of the world. Use them as instruments of righteousness to defeat the plans of the devil.

Lord, we plead the power of the blood of Jesus, asking You to manifest Your power and glory. We entreat You on behalf of the citizens in these countries on both sides of this conflict. They have experienced pain and heartache; they are victims of the devil's strategies to steal, kill, and destroy. We pray that they will come to know Jesus Who came to give us life, and life more abundantly.

We stand in the gap for the people of the war-torn, devil-overrun land. We expect an overflowing of Your goodness and glory in the lives of those for whom we are praying. May they call upon Your name and be saved.

You, Lord, make known Your salvation; Your righteousness You openly show in the sight of the nations.

Father, provide for and protect the families of our armed forces. Preserve marriages, cause the hearts of the parents to turn toward their children, and the hearts of the children to turn toward the fathers and mothers. We plead the blood of Jesus over our troops and their families. Provide a support system to undergird, uplift, and edify those who have been left to raise children by themselves. Jesus has been made unto these parents wisdom, righteousness, and sanctification.

201

Through Your Holy Spirit, comfort the lonely and strengthen the weary.

Father, we are looking forward to that day when the whole earth shall be filled with the knowledge of the Lord as the waters cover the sea.

In Jesus' name, amen.

Scripture References

Ephesians 6:12 MESSAGE	Psalm 98:2 AMP
Colossians 2:15	Malachi 4:6
John 10:10	1 Corinthians 1:30
Ezekiel 22:30	Isaiah 11:9
Acts 2:21	

A portion of this prayer was taken from a letter dated January 22, 1996, written by Kenneth Copeland of Kenneth Copeland Ministries in Fort Worth, Texas, and sent to his partners. Used by permission.

✒ *Sixty-Seven* ✒

The Nation and People of Israel

Lord, You will not cast off nor spurn Your people, neither will You abandon Your heritage. You have regard for the covenant [You made with Abraham]. Father, remember Your covenant with Abraham, Isaac, and Jacob.

Father, we pray for the peace of Jerusalem. May they prosper who love you [the Holy City]. May peace be within your walls and prosperity within your palaces! For our brethren and companions' sake, we will now say, Peace be within you! For the sake of the house of the Lord our God, we will seek, inquire for, and require your good.

Father, we thank You for bringing the people of Israel into unity with each other, and for bringing Your Church (both Jew and Gentile) into oneness — one new man. Thank You for the peace treaties with Israel's former enemies. May these treaties be used for good to make way for the good news of the Gospel as we prepare for the coming of our Messiah.

We intercede for those who have become callously indifferent (blinded, hardened, and made insensible to the Gospel). We pray that they will not fall to their utter spiritual ruin. It was through their false step and transgression that salvation has come to the Gentiles. Now, we ask that the eyes of their understanding be enlightened that they may know the Messiah Who will make Himself known to all of Israel.

We ask You to strengthen the house of Judah and save the house of Joseph. Thank You, Father, for restoring them because You have compassion on them. They will be as though You had not rejected them, for You are the Lord their God, and You will answer them. We thank You for Your great mercy and love to them and to us, in the name of Yeshua, our Messiah.

Father, thank You for saving Israel, and gathering them from the nations, that they may give thanks to Your holy name and glory in Your praise. Praise be to You, Lord, the God of Israel, from everlasting to everlasting. Let all the people say, "Amen!" Praise the Lord.

In Jesus' name, amen.

Scripture References

Psalm 94:14 AMP

Psalm 74:20 AMP

Leviticus 46:22

Psalm 122:6-9 AMP

Ephesians 2:14 AMP

Romans 11:7 AMP

Romans 11:11 AMP

Ephesians 1:18

Zechariah 10:6,12 NIV

Psalm 106:47,48 NIV

Praying the Word
by Germaine Copeland

...The earnest (heartfelt, continued) prayer of a righteous man makes tremendous power available — dynamic in its working.

James 5:16 AMP

Prayer is fellowshiping with the Father — a vital, personal contact with God Who is more than enough. We are to be in constant communion with Him:

For the eyes of the Lord are upon the righteous — those who are upright and in right standing with God — and His ears are attentive (open) to their prayer....

1 Peter 3:12 AMP

Prayer is not to be a religious form with no power. It is to be effective and accurate and bring *results*. God watches over His Word to perform it. (Jer. 1:12.)

Prayer that brings results must be based on God's Word.

For the Word that God speaks is alive and full of power — making it active, operative, energizing and effective; it is sharper than any two-edged sword, penetrating to the dividing line of the breath of life (soul) and

[the immortal] spirit, and of joints and marrow [that is, of the deepest parts of our nature] exposing and sifting and analyzing and judging the very thoughts and purposes of the heart.

Hebrews 4:12 AMP

Prayer is this "living" Word in our mouths. Our mouths must speak forth faith, for faith is what pleases God. (Heb. 11:6.) We hold His Word up to Him in prayer, and our Father sees Himself in His Word.

God's Word is our contact with Him. We put Him in remembrance of His Word (Isa. 43:26) placing a demand on His ability in the name of our Lord Jesus. We remind Him that He supplies all of our needs according to His riches in glory by Christ Jesus. (Phil. 4:19.) That Word does not return to Him void — without producing any effect, useless — but it *shall* accomplish that which He pleases and purposes, and it shall prosper in the thing for which He sent it. (Isa. 55:11.) Hallelujah!

God did *not* leave us without His thoughts and His ways for we have His Word — His bond. God instructs us to call Him, and He will answer and show us great and mighty things. (Jer. 33:3.) Prayer is to be exciting — not drudgery.

It takes someone to pray. God moves as we pray in faith — believing. He says that His eyes run to and fro throughout the whole earth to show Himself strong in behalf of those whose hearts are blameless toward Him. (2 Chron. 16:9.) We are blameless. (Eph. 1:4.) We are His very own children. (Eph. 1:5.) We are His righteousness in Christ Jesus. (2 Cor. 5:21.) He tells us to come boldly to the throne of grace and *obtain* mercy and find grace to help in time of need — appropriate and well-timed help. (Heb. 4:16.) Praise the Lord!

The prayer armor is for every believer, every member of the Body of Christ, who will put it on and walk in it, for the weapons of our warfare are *not carnal* but mighty through God for the pulling down of the strongholds of the enemy (Satan, the god of this world, and all his demonic forces). Spiritual warfare takes place in prayer. (2 Cor. 10:4, Eph. 6:12,18.)

There are many different kinds of prayer, such as the prayer of thanksgiving and praise, the prayer of dedication and worship, and the prayer that changes *things* (not God). All prayer involves a time of fellowshiping with the Father.

In Ephesians 6, we are instructed to take the sword of the Spirit which is the Word of God and **pray at all times — on every occasion, in every season — in the**

Spirit, with all [manner of] prayer and entreaty (Eph. 6:18 AMP).

In 1 Timothy 2 we are admonished and urged that **petitions, prayers, intercessions and thanksgivings be offered on behalf of all men** (1 Tim 2:1 AMP). *Prayer is our responsibility.*

Prayer must be the foundation of every Christian endeavor. Any failure is a prayer failure. We are not to be ignorant concerning God's Word. God desires for His people to be successful, to be filled with a full, deep, and clear knowledge of His will (His Word), and to bear fruit in every good work. (Col. 1:9-13.) We then bring honor and glory to Him. (John 15:8.) He desires that we know how to pray for **the prayer of the upright is his delight** (Prov. 15:8).

208

Our Father has not left us helpless. Not only has He given us His Word, but also He has given us the Holy Spirit to help our infirmities when we know not how to pray as we ought. (Rom. 8:26.) Praise God! Our Father has provided His people with every possible avenue to insure their complete and total victory in this life in the name of our Lord Jesus. (1 John 5:3-5.)

We pray to the Father, in the name of Jesus, through the Holy Spirit, according to the Word!

Using God's Word on purpose, specifically, in prayer is one means of prayer, and it is a most effective and accurate means. Jesus said, **The words (truths) that I have been speaking to you are spirit and life** (John 6:63 AMP).

When Jesus faced Satan in the wilderness, He said, "It is written...it is written...it is written." We are to live, be upheld, and sustained by every Word that proceeds from the mouth of God. (Matt. 4:4.)

James, by the Spirit, admonishes that we do not have, because we do not ask. We ask and receive not, because we ask amiss. (James 4:2,3.) We must heed that admonishment now for we are to become experts in prayer rightly dividing the Word of Truth. (2 Tim. 2:15.)

Using the Word in prayer is *not* taking it out of context, for His Word in us is the key to answered prayer — to prayer that brings results. He is able to do exceeding abundantly above all we ask or think, according to the power that works in us. (Eph. 3:20.) The power lies within God's Word. It is anointed by the Holy Spirit. The Spirit of God does not lead us apart from the Word, for the Word is of the Spirit of God. We apply that Word personally to ourselves and to others — not adding to or taking from it — in the name of Jesus. We apply the Word to the *now* —to those things, circumstances, and situations facing each of us *now*.

Paul was very specific and definite in his praying. The first chapters of Ephesians, Philippians, Colossians, and 2 Thessalonians are examples of how Paul prayed for believers. There are numerous others. *Search them out.* Paul wrote under the inspiration of the Holy Spirit. We can use these Spirit-given prayers today!

In 2 Corinthians 1:11, 2 Corinthians 9:14, and Philippians 1:4, we see examples of how believers prayed one for another — putting others first in their prayer life with *joy.* Our faith does work by love. (Gal. 5:6.) We grow spiritually as we reach out to help others — praying for and with them and holding out to them the Word of Life. (Phil. 2:16.)

Man is a spirit, he has a soul, and he lives in a body. (1 Thess. 5:23.) In order to operate successfully, each of these three parts must be fed properly. The soul or intellect feeds on intellectual food to produce intellectual strength. The body feeds on physical food to produce physical strength. The spirit — the heart or inward man — is the real you, the part that has been reborn in Christ Jesus. It must feed on spirit food which is God's Word in order to produce and develop faith. As we feast upon God's Word, our minds become renewed with His Word, and we have a fresh mental and spiritual attitude. (Eph. 4:23,24.)

Likewise, we are to present our bodies a living sacrifice, holy, acceptable unto God (Rom. 12:1) and not let that body dominate us but bring it into subjection to the spirit man. (1 Cor. 9:27.) God's Word is healing and health to all our flesh. (Prov. 4:22.) Therefore, God's Word affects each part of us — spirit, soul and body. We become vitally united to the Father, to Jesus, and to the Holy Spirit — one with Them. (John 16:13-15, John 17:21, Col. 2:10.)

God's Word, this spirit food, takes root in our hearts, is formed by the tongue, and is spoken out of our mouths. This is creative power. The spoken Word works as we confess it and then apply the action to it.

Be doers of the Word, and not hearers only, deceiving your own selves. (James 1:22.) Faith without works or corresponding action is *dead*. (James 2:17.) Don't be mental assenters — those who agree that the Bible is true but never act on it. *Real faith is acting on God's Word now.* We cannot build faith without practicing the Word. We cannot develop an effective prayer life that is anything but empty words unless God's Word actually has a part in our lives. We are to hold fast to our *confession* of the Word's truthfulness. Our Lord Jesus is the High Priest of our confession (Heb. 3:1), and He is the Guarantee of a better agreement — a more excellent and advantageous covenant. (Heb. 7:22.)

Prayer does not cause faith to work, but faith causes prayer to work. Therefore, any prayer problem is a

211

problem of doubt — doubting the integrity of the Word and the ability of God to stand behind His promises or the statements of fact in the Word.

We can spend fruitless hours in prayer if our hearts are not prepared beforehand. Preparation of the heart, the spirit, comes from meditation in the Father's Word, meditation on who we are in Christ, what He is to us, and what the Holy Spirit can mean to us as we become God-inside minded. As God told Joshua (Josh. 1:8), as we meditate on the Word day and night, and do according to all that is written, then shall we make our way prosperous and have good success. We are to attend to God's Word, submit to His sayings, keep them in the center of our hearts, and put away contrary talk. (Prov. 4:20-24.)

When we use God's Word in prayer, this is *not* something we just rush through uttering once, and we are finished. Do *not* be mistaken. There is nothing "magical" nor "manipulative" about it — no set pattern or device in order to satisfy what we want or think out of our flesh. Instead we are holding God's Word before Him. We confess what He says belongs to us.

We expect His divine intervention while we choose not to look at the things that are seen but at the things that are unseen, for the things that are seen are subject to change. (2 Cor. 4:18.)

Prayer based upon the Word rises above the senses, contacts the Author of the Word and sets His spiritual laws into motion. It is not just saying prayers that gets results, but it is spending time with the Father, learning His wisdom, drawing on His strength, being filled with His quietness, and basking in His love that bring results to our prayers. Praise the Lord!

* * *

The prayers in this book are designed to teach and train you in the art of personal confession and intercessory prayer. As you pray them, you will be reinforcing the prayer armor which we have been instructed to put on in Ephesians 6:11. The fabric from which the armor is made is the Word of God. We are to live by every word that proceeds from the mouth of God. We desire the whole counsel of God, because we know it changes us. By receiving that counsel, you will be **...transformed (changed) by the [entire] renewal of your mind — by its new ideals and its new attitude — so that you may prove [for yourselves] what is the good and acceptable and perfect will of God, even the thing which is good and acceptable and perfect [in His sight for you]** (Rom. 12:2 AMP).

The prayers of personal confession of the Word of God for yourself can also be used as intercessory prayers for others by simply praying them in the third person, changing the pronouns *I* or *we* to the name of the person or persons for whom you are interceding and adjusting the verbs accordingly.

The prayers of intercession have blanks in which you (individually or as a group) are to fill in the spaces with the name of the person(s) for whom you are praying. These prayers of intercession can likewise be made into prayers of personal confession for yourself (or your group) by inserting your own name(s) and the proper personal pronouns in the appropriate places.

An often-asked question is: "How many times should I pray the same prayer?"

The answer is simple: you pray until you know that the answer is fixed in your heart. After that, you need to repeat the prayer whenever adverse circumstances or long delays cause you to be tempted to doubt that your prayer has been heard and your request granted.

The Word of God is your weapon against the temptation to lose heart and grow weary in your prayer life. When that Word of promise becomes fixed in your heart, you will find yourself praising, giving glory to God for the answer, even when the only evidence you have of that answer is your own faith.

Another question often asked is: "When we repeat prayers more than once, aren't we praying 'vain repetitions'?"

Obviously, such people are referring to the admonition of Jesus when He told His disciples: **And when you pray do not (multiply words, repeating the same ones over and over, and) heap up phrases as the Gentiles do, for they think they will be heard for their much speaking** (Matt. 6:7 AMP). Praying the Word of God is not praying the kind of prayer that the "heathen" pray. You will note in 1 Kings 18:25-29 the manner of prayer that was offered to the gods who could not hear. That is not the way you and I pray. The words that we speak are not vain, but they are spirit and life, and mighty through God to the pulling down of strongholds. We have a God Whose eyes are over the righteous and Whose ears are open to us: when we pray, He hears us.

You are the righteousness of God in Christ Jesus, and your prayers will avail much. They will bring salvation to the sinner, deliverance to the oppressed, healing to the sick, and prosperity to the poor. They will usher in the next move of God in the earth. In addition to affecting outward circumstances and other people, your prayers will also have an effect upon you.

In the very process of praying, your life will be changed as you go from faith to faith and from glory to glory.

As a Christian, your first priority is to love the Lord your God with your entire being, and your neighbor as

About the Author

Germaine Griffin Copeland, founder and president of Word Ministries, Inc., is the author of the Prayers That Avail Much Family Books. Her writings provide scriptural prayer instruction to help you pray effectively for those things that concern you and your family and for other prayer assignments. Her teachings on prayer, the personal growth of the intercessor, emotional healing and related subjects have brought understanding, hope, healing and liberty to the discouraged and emotionally wounded. She is a woman of prayer and praise whose highest form of worship is the study of God's Word. Her greatest desire is to know God.

Word Ministries, Inc. is a prayer and teaching ministry. Germaine believes that God has called her to teach the practical application of the Word of Truth for successful, victorious living. After years of searching diligently for truth, and trying again and again to come out of depression, she decided that she was a mistake. Out of the depths of despair she called upon the name of the Lord, and the Light of God's presence invaded the room where she was sitting.

It was in that moment that she experienced the warmth of God's love; old things passed away and she felt brand new. She discovered a motivation for living — life had purpose. Living in the presence of God she has found unconditional love and acceptance, healing for crippled emotions, contentment that overcomes depression, peace in the midst of adverse circumstances, and grace for developing healthy relationships. The on-going process of transformation evolved into praying for others, and the prayer of intercession became her prayer focus.

Germaine is the daughter of Reverend A. H. "Buck" Griffin and the late Donnis Brock Griffin. She and her husband, Everette, have four children, five grandchildren and two great-grandchildren. Germaine and Everette reside in Sandy Springs, a suburb of Atlanta, Georgia.

Word Ministries' offices are located in Historic Roswell, 38 Sloan Street, Roswell, Georgia 30075. Telephone: 770-518-1065

You may contact
Word Ministries
by writing

Word Ministries, Inc.
38 Sloan Street
Roswell, Georgia 30075
or calling 770-518-1065

*Please include
your prayer requests
and comments when you write.*

The Harrison House Vision

Proclaiming the truth and the power

Of the Gospel of Jesus Christ

With excellence;

Challenging Christians to

Live victoriously,

Grow spiritually,

Know God intimately.